Fiqh al-Muwāzanāt

The Jurisprudence of Weighing Benefits & Harms

SULEIMAN HANI

Foreword by DR. HATEM AL-HAJ

Waymark Publications
ISBN 978-1-969358-03-6

Website: imamsuleiman.com
Ordering Information:
Special discounts are available on bulk purchases by bookstores, educational institutions, wholesalers, mosques, and others. For details, contact the author's administration at the website above.

waymarkpublications.com

CONTENTS

Foreword

Islamic law has always embodied both permanence and dynamism: permanence in its divine foundations, and dynamism in its application across times and places. The juristic discipline of fiqh al-muwāzanāt—the weighing and balancing of competing benefits and harms—is a striking example of this dual character. Its essence is the recognition that the Sharīʿah does not compel believers into rigidity or contradiction, but provides a framework for deliberation when pure options are unavailable and when fidelity to divine intent demands prioritization.

Across centuries, scholars confronted circumstances unforeseen by earlier generations, yet always returned to the principle that the Sharīʿah was revealed to secure benefit (jalb al-maṣāliḥ) and avert harm (darʾ al-mafāsid). Imām Ibn al-Qayyim (rA) captured this spirit with penetrating clarity when he wrote that "the Sharīʿah is founded upon wisdom and the welfare of people in this world and the next. In its entirety it is justice, mercy, benefit, and wisdom. Every matter that departs from justice to oppression, from mercy to cruelty, from benefit to harm, and from wisdom to futility, is not part of the Sharīʿah, even if it is inserted into it by interpretation."[1]

This recognition—that law is not an abstraction but a living instrument of justice—forms the foundation of fiqh al-muwāzanāt. And it is further exemplified by Imām Ibn Taymiyyah (rA), who explained that the Sharīʿah came to secure benefits and perfect them, to prevent harms and reduce them, to give preference to the greater of two goods when both cannot be attained, and to repel the greater of two evils by bearing the lesser of them.2

It is not surprising, then, that Imām Ibn Taymiyyah (rA) dedicated an entire chapter under the title "A Comprehensive Section on the Conflict Between Good Deeds and Evil Deeds, or Both Together" (*Faṣl jāmiʿ fī taʿāruḍ al-ḥasanāt aw al-sayyiʾāt aw humā jamīʿan*) to this very subject—an extended treatment that remains one of the most systematic discussions of weighing and

---

[1] *Iʿlām al-Muwaqqiʿīn*, 3:11, Dār al-Kutub al-ʿIlmiyyah, 1st ed., 1991.

[2] *Majmūʿ al-Fatāwā, 20:48, Majmaʿ al-Malik Fahd li-Ṭibāʿat al-Muṣḥaf al-Sharīf, Madīnah, 1425 AH.*

prioritization in our tradition. The present work draws upon these insights and the broader Taymiyyan legacy in this respect. It also masterfully and seamlessly draws on the wider juristic tradition shaped by great imams such as al-Qarāfī (rA), al-ʿIzz ibn ʿAbd al-Salām (rA), and al-Shāṭibī (rA), along with many others who affirmed this balancing as a central juristic method across the centuries. In addition, the work explicitly acknowledges the contemporary contributions of Shaykh Yūsuf al-Qaraḍāwī (rA), particularly his writings on fiqh al-awlawiyyāt and fiqh al-wāqiʿ, as important complements in the modern articulation of this methodology.

The book before you, ***The Fiqh of Muwāzanāt: Principles and Guidelines***, is a systematic effort to bring this methodology to bear on contemporary realities. It clarifies the essential prerequisites for sound balancing—knowledge of objectives, causes, context, consequences, and priorities—before unfolding into typologies, applications, and strategic principles. In doing so, it also addresses the interrelated disciplines without which this field cannot function properly, such as fiqh al-wāqiʿ (the jurisprudence of context and reality), fiqh al-maʾālāt (the consideration of consequences), fiqh al-awlawiyyāt (the jurisprudence of priorities), and other methodological tools that jurists have historically relied upon to preserve the higher purposes of the law.

What distinguishes this contribution is not only its grounding in the classical legacy but also its attentiveness to modern challenges. The author demonstrates how fiqh al-muwāzanāt illuminates questions of political participation, artificial intelligence, and digital transformations of family and community. These are not abstract puzzles but lived realities for Muslims today—whether in the West as minorities navigating secular democracies, or in Muslim-majority lands grappling with global systems, technological change, and competing social pressures.

It is my hope that this book will serve as a resource for scholars, imams, students, and thoughtful Muslims who wish to cultivate the disciplined insight required to navigate our complex age. In it, readers will find not only an introduction to a vital juristic methodology but also a living testimony to the continuing relevance of the Islamic tradition.

If I may stress one final point, it is that no methodology, however sophisticated, can replace the spiritual and moral cultivation of the jurist or leader who seeks to apply it. The balancing of benefits and harms is not a mechanical exercise of intellect alone. It requires sincerity of purpose, purity of intention, and a heart illuminated by the remembrance of God. For the one who engages in fiqh al-muwāzanāt must not only possess knowledge of texts, maxims, and contexts, but also the correct qaṣd—to seek God's pleasure and the preservation of His religion. And he must recognize his utter dependence upon divine assistance, for without it, even the soundest reasoning may falter.

It is in this marriage of rigorous method and upright spirit that fiqh al-muwāzanāt becomes not merely an academic framework, but a living path by which the Muslim community can navigate its challenges with wisdom, justice, and fidelity to revelation.

May God's blessings and peace be upon Muḥammad, and all praise belongs to God, Lord of the worlds.

Dr. Hatem Al-Haj

Introduction

In an era of unprecedented complexity, Muslim communities worldwide confront challenges that defy simple resolution. From artificial intelligence systems making consequential decisions about human lives to digital platforms transforming the most intimate aspects of social interaction, from political landscapes demanding sophisticated navigation to bioethical dilemmas unknown to previous generations, contemporary Muslims face scenarios where multiple Islamic principles appear to conflict, where benefits and harms intertwine inextricably, and where the path of religious fidelity seems anything but clear.[3]

It is precisely for such moments that Islamic jurisprudence developed *fiqh al-muwāzanāt*—the sophisticated methodology of balancing competing interests, benefits, and harms according to divine guidance and prophetic wisdom. While the principles underlying this approach permeate classical Islamic scholarship, their systematic articulation as a distinct discipline responds to contemporary needs for structured frameworks that can address complexity without sacrificing authenticity.

The Nature and Scope of This Work

Fiqh al-muwāzanāt represents a methodological approach within Islamic jurisprudence concerned with the weighing of benefits (*maṣāliḥ*) against harms (*mafāsid*) when multiple considerations are at stake.[4] As defined by contemporary scholars, it involves the comparison and preference among benefits, among harms, and between conflicting benefits and harms, so as to

---

[3] For the purpose of this book, artificial intelligence refers to machine-based systems that, for explicit or implicit objectives, infer from the inputs they receive how to generate outputs such as predictions, content, recommendations, or decisions that may influence physical or virtual environments. This definition aligns with the updated OECD formulation, which has become influential in contemporary AI governance. See Organisation for Economic Co-operation and Development, *Recommendation of the Council on Artificial Intelligence*, OECD/LEGAL/0449, adopted May 22, 2019, amended May 3, 2024; National Institute of Standards and Technology, *Artificial Intelligence Risk Management Framework (AI RMF 1.0)*, NIST AI 100-1 (Gaithersburg, MD: NIST, January 2023); UNESCO, *Recommendation on the Ethics of Artificial Intelligence* (Paris: UNESCO, 2021).

[4] Yūsuf al-Qaraḍāwī, *Fī Fiqh al-Awlawiyyāt: Dirāsah Jadīdah fī Ḍaw' al-Qur'ān wa al-Sunnah* [Jurisprudence of Priorities: A New Study in Light of the Quran and Sunnah] (Cairo: Maktabat Wahbah, 1996).

advance or delay that which deserves advancement or delay.[5] This discipline stands closely connected to the broader Islamic legal objectives (*maqāṣid al-sharīʿah*) and provides principles for resolving tensions between competing interests, particularly in complex situations where simple solutions prove elusive. As Ibn al-Qayyim eloquently stated, the foundation of the Sharīʿah is wisdom and the safeguarding of people's interests in this world and the next; in its entirety, it is justice, mercy, benefit, and wisdom.[6]

This book presents the first comprehensive English-language treatment of *fiqh al-muwāzanāt* as a systematic methodology for contemporary Islamic legal reasoning. Moving beyond scattered precedents and isolated examples, it articulates the essential conditions, typologies, and strategic principles that enable qualified scholars and institutional bodies to navigate complex scenarios with methodological rigor and spiritual insight.

A Framework for Contemporary Challenges

The work unfolds across seven chapters, each building upon previous foundations while advancing toward practical application:

Chapter 1 traces the intellectual genealogy of *fiqh al-muwāzanāt*, demonstrating how contemporary systematization emerges from centuries of Islamic legal development while responding to unprecedented modern complexities.

Chapter 2 establishes the necessity and objectives of this methodology, articulating why contemporary contexts demand sophisticated frameworks for balancing competing considerations across individual, communal, and civilizational dimensions.

Chapter 3 presents the five essential conditions required for competent engagement in *fiqh al-muwāzanāt*: mastery of Islamic legal objectives (*maqāṣid*), verification of effective causes (*taḥqīq al-manāṭ*), understanding contemporary contexts (*fiqh al-wāqiʿ*), considering consequences (*iʿtibār al-maʾālāt*), and establishing priorities (*fiqh al-awlawiyyāt*).

Chapter 4 examines the three fundamental typologies of balancing: between competing benefits, between conflicting harms, and between benefits and harms, providing systematic approaches to each category with classical and contemporary examples.

---

[5] ʿAbd Allāh Yaḥyā al-Kamālī, *Taʾṣīl fiqh al-muwāzanāt* [Establishing the Jurisprudence of Balancing] (Beirut: Dār Ibn Ḥazm, 2000).

[6] Ibn al-Qayyim al-Jawziyyah, *Iʿlām al-Muwaqqiʿīn ʿan Rabb al-ʿĀlamīn*, ed. Muḥammad ʿAbd al-Salām Ibrāhīm, 4 vols. (Beirut: Dār al-Kutub al-ʿIlmiyyah, 1991), 3/11.

Chapter 5 develops strategic principles for implementation, including temporal urgency, the relationship between goals and means, graduated approaches, and the jurisprudence of lesser harm.

Chapter 6 addresses advanced methodological considerations, exploring what occurs when systematic analysis reaches its limits and alternative approaches become necessary.

Chapter 7 synthesizes the entire framework while projecting future trajectories for institutional development, interdisciplinary integration, and pedagogical advancement.

Three Case Studies

Throughout these chapters, three contemporary domains serve as recurring case studies, demonstrating how classical principles address new challenges:

1. **Political Participation in Democratic Systems**
   How do Muslims navigate electoral engagement when candidates support policies conflicting with Islamic values? What frameworks guide coalition-building with groups holding diverse worldviews? How should communities respond when institutions become systemically corrupted?

2. **Artificial Intelligence Governance**
   As AI systems are increasingly adopted, how do Islamic principles guide their development and deployment? What balancing occurs between efficiency gains and risks of perpetuating injustice? How do we preserve human dignity and divine wisdom in an algorithmic age?

3. **Digital Transformation of Social Relations**
   When platforms reshape how Muslims seek spouses for marriage, form communities, and transmit knowledge, what principles guide engagement? How do we balance accessibility with authenticity, connection with protection, innovation with tradition?

For Whom This Work Is Written

This book primarily addresses scholars, imams, students of Islamic knowledge, and institutional leaders who bear responsibility for guiding Muslim communities through contemporary challenges. It assumes familiarity with Islamic legal terminology and comfort with sophisticated theoretical discussions. Yet its implications extend to every thoughtful Muslim seeking to understand how divine guidance engages modern complexity.

For scholarly councils and institutional bodies, the work provides systematic frameworks for collective deliberation. For individual scholars, it offers methodological tools for addressing unprecedented questions. For advanced students, it demonstrates how classical Islamic sciences remain vibrantly relevant to contemporary life.

A Living Tradition

The Prophet ﷺ promised that Allah would send renewers (*mujaddidūn*) to revive this religion for each generation. In our age of accelerating change and multiplying complexity, such renewal requires not merely individual insight but systematic methodologies enabling continuous adaptation while preserving authentic principles. *Fiqh al-muwāzanāt* represents one essential component of this broader renewal, a framework through which eternal divine guidance engages temporal human complexity.

This work emerges from recognition that simplistic approaches, whether rigid literalism or unprincipled accommodation, fail to honor either divine wisdom or human dignity. Between these extremes lies the path of principled flexibility, systematic reasoning, and collective wisdom that *fiqh al-muwāzanāt* embodies.

As you embark upon this intellectual journey, know that you engage with more than academic theory. You encounter a living methodology through which the Islamic tradition demonstrates its continued capacity to provide meaningful guidance for humanity's most complex challenges. May this work serve as both scholarly resource and practical guide for all who seek to live faithfully in our beautifully complex world.

A special note of gratitude to the scholars, teachers, colleagues, and students of knowledge who reviewed this work individually and at the AMJA conference where this was presented to over 500 Imams, teachers, and students of knowledge. May Allah accept it from you as a continuous charity. In particular, gratitude to Dr. Hatem Al Haj and Sh. Omar Hedroug for their detailed and thorough review of the manuscript.

Suleiman Hani

1

Contemporary Scholarship & Methodological Development

The systematic articulation of fiqh al-muwāzanāt as a distinct jurisprudential discipline represents the culmination of methodological developments spanning over a millennium of Islamic legal scholarship. While the principles of balancing interests (*muwāzanat al-maṣāliḥ wa al-mafāsid*) were operationalized throughout Islamic legal history, their explicit systematization reflects contemporary scholarly responses to unprecedented challenges facing Muslim communities in pluralistic societies.

Related Terminology and Conceptual Framework

Understanding fiqh al-muwāzanāt and its history first requires clarity regarding several interconnected jurisprudential concepts that form its methodological foundation. For instance, fiqh al-awlawiyyāt (the jurisprudence of priorities) represents a parallel discipline that deals with the ordering of benefits and harms in the absence of direct conflict. It constitutes the closest designation to fiqh al-muwāzanāt, as both disciplines concern themselves with the systematic evaluation and ranking of competing considerations according to Islamic legal principles. As expressed by Dr. Yusuf al-Qaradawi, *fiqh al-muwāzanāt* itself may be seen as an entire subdiscipline and constituent principle of the fiqh of priorities.[7] Other related terms include fiqh al-wāqiʿ, fiqh al-maṣāliḥ, fiqh al-ḍarūriyyāt, and fiqh al-maʾālāt, among other subdisciplines.

Fiqh al-Wāqiʿ (the jurisprudence of contemporary realities) constitutes a related field of study that focuses on recognizing the influential descriptions and prevailing conditions that necessitate applying specific Sharʿī rulings. This discipline requires a profound understanding of the situation in which the

[7] Al-Qaraḍāwī, *Fī Fiqh al-Awlawiyyāt*, 45-123.

ummah finds itself, considering present circumstances within one region and the broader international context. This is considered one of the conditions, and branches, of effective engagement with fiqh al-muwāzanāt.

Fiqh al-Maṣāliḥ (the jurisprudence of benefits/interests) derives its name from the subject matter of this discipline, which encompasses both benefits (maṣāliḥ) and harms (mafāsid). The terminology emphasizes "benefits" following the principle of highlighting the predominant aspect, though the discipline necessarily addresses both positive and negative considerations.

Fiqh al-Ḍarūriyyāt (the jurisprudence of fundamental necessities) emphasizes the highest level of interests considered in balancing factors, namely, the "essential necessities" (ḍarūriyyāt). While other interests remain significant, the essential necessities receive explicit priority due to their fundamental importance in Islamic legal reasoning.

Fiqh al-Maʾālāt (the jurisprudence of consequences) requires consideration of the likely outcomes of actions rather than merely their immediate effects. Ibn al-Qayyim emphasized that "the muftī must not issue a fatwā unless he considers the consequences of his opinion."[1] This is considered one of the conditions, and branches, of effective engagement with fiqh al-muwāzanāt.[8]

Typologies and Revelatory Foundations

The concept of *fiqh al-muwāzanāt* finds firm grounding in numerous Qurʾānic verses and Prophetic traditions that establish principles for prioritizing interests, averting harm, and evaluating consequences. These scriptural sources demonstrate the Lawgiver's consistent emphasis on preventing greater harm, even when such prevention requires tolerating lesser harm or forgoing certain benefits. *Fiqh al-muwāzanāt* is conventionally categorized into three distinct methodological types, explored in great detail later in this book: 1) The balancing of benefits (muwāzanat al-maṣāliḥ), 2) The balancing of harms (muwāzanat al-mafāsid), and 3) The balancing between benefits and harms (muwāzanat al-maṣāliḥ wa al-mafāsid).

Classical Foundations

Three classical scholars established the foundational architecture for contemporary muwāzanāt methodology. Al-ʿIzz ibn ʿAbd al-Salām (d. 660 AH/1262 CE) provided systematic criteria for distinguishing legitimate from

[8] See: Ibn al-Qayyim, *Iʿlām al-Muwaqqiʿīn ʿan Rabb al-ʿĀlamīn*, 4:157.

illegitimate *maṣlaḥah* through his seminal work *Qawāʿid al-Aḥkām fī Maṣāliḥ al-Anām.*[9] His fundamental principle that "repelling harm takes precedence over securing benefits" (*darʾ al-mafāsid muqaddam ʿalā jalb al-maṣāliḥ*) established the framework that prioritizes prevention of corruption over achievement of positive outcomes when both cannot be simultaneously accomplished.[10] His taxonomical contributions, categorizing benefits and harms according to scope, certainty, and temporal dimensions, provided analytical tools that contemporary scholars continue to refine and apply.

Abū Isḥāq al-Shāṭibī (d. 790 AH/1388 CE) revolutionized Islamic legal methodology through his systematic articulation of maqāṣid al-sharīʿah in *Al-Muwāfaqāt.*[11] His tripartite categorization of legal objectives into necessities (*darūriyyāt*), needs (*ḥājiyyāt*), and improvements (*taḥsīniyyāt*) provided unprecedented methodological precision for resolving conflicts between competing interests. Crucially, his recognition that the five essential necessities could themselves conflict and require systematic prioritization anticipated contemporary challenges addressed through fiqh al-muwāzanāt.[12]

Ibn Taymiyyah (d. 728 AH/1328 CE) provided essential methodological tools through his sophisticated treatment of analogical reasoning and the verification of effective causes (*taḥqīq al-manāṭ*).[13] His tripartite framework, *tanqīḥ al-manāṭ, takhrīj al-manāṭ, and taḥqīq al-manāṭ*, enables contemporary scholars to determine when classical rulings apply to novel circumstances without inappropriate mechanical application. His assertion that the Sharīʿah came to achieve benefits and perfect them, to prevent harms and reduce them, provides theological foundation for systematic interest-balancing grounded in divine wisdom rather than mere utilitarian calculation.[14]

---

[9] ʿIzz al-Dīn ʿAbd al-Salām, *Qawāʿid al-Aḥkām fī Maṣāliḥ al-Anām* (Beirut: Dār al-Kutub al-ʿIlmiyya, 1999).

[10] This principle provided a methodological foundation for the complex calculations that characterize contemporary muwāzanāt applications.

[11] Al-Shāṭibī, *Al-Muwāfaqāt fī Uṣūl al-Sharīʿa*, ed. ʿAbd Allah Darrāz, 4 vols. (Beirut: Dār al-Kutub al-ʿIlmiyya, 2003).

[12] His methodological emphasis on understanding the "wisdom" (ḥikmah) underlying specific legal rulings provided foundation for contemporary approaches that distinguish between unchanging principles and contextually variable applications.

[13] Ibn Taymiyyah, *Majmūʿ al-Fatāwā* [Collected Fatwas], ed. ʿAbd al-Raḥmān ibn Qāsim, 37 vols. (al-Manṣūrah: Dār al-Wafāʾ, 2005).

[14] His sophisticated treatment of political questions in al-Siyāsah al-Sharʿiyyah demonstrates practical application to governance challenges paralleling contemporary Muslim political engagement.

Modern Systematic Development

Dr. Yūsuf al-Qaraḍāwī (d. 2022) proved instrumental in developing fiqh al-muwāzanāt as a distinct jurisprudential approach through his comprehensive scholarly production spanning over six decades. His seminal work *Fī Fiqh al-Awlawiyyāt* (On the Jurisprudence of Priorities) provided the first systematic treatment of priority-determination in contemporary Islamic legal reasoning.[15]

Al-Qaraḍāwī's methodological contributions encompassed both theoretical foundation and practical application. His articulation of the relationship between *fiqh al-awlawiyyāt* (jurisprudence of priorities), *fiqh al-wāqiʿ* (jurisprudence of reality), and *fiqh al-muwāzanāt* provided integrated framework for contemporary *ijtihād* that addresses the complex interdependencies characterizing modern social and political challenges.[16]

His treatment of Muslim minority jurisprudence (*fiqh al-aqalliyyāt*) in works such as *Al-Siyāsah al-Sharʿiyyah* demonstrated practical application of interest-balancing principles to challenges facing Muslim communities in pluralistic societies, providing crucial precedent for contemporary American Muslim applications.[17]

Contemporary Methodological Renaissance

The development of systematic fiqh al-muwāzanāt occurs within a broader contemporary renaissance in Islamic legal methodology, as Muslim scholars worldwide grapple with applying classical jurisprudential principles to unprecedented modern contexts. This methodological revival encompasses diverse geographical, institutional, and intellectual contexts while demonstrating remarkable convergence around the necessity for more sophisticated frameworks for contemporary legal reasoning.

North American Scholarly Contributions

The International Institute of Islamic Thought and Methodological Reform

Ṭāhā Jābir al-ʿAlwānī's (d. 2016) foundational work through the International Institute of Islamic Thought represents perhaps the most systematic attempt to address methodological challenges facing Muslim minorities in pluralistic societies. His concept of *fiqh al-aqalliyyāt* (jurisprudence of minorities) directly parallels concerns addressed through fiqh al-muwāzanāt, particularly

---

[15] Al-Qaraḍāwī, *Fī Fiqh al-Awlawiyyāt*, 45-123.
[16] Al-Qaraḍāwī, *Al-Siyāsah al-Sharʿiyyah* [The Legal Political System] (Cairo: Dār al-Shurūq, 2006).
[17] Ibid., 234-289.

regarding the balance between Islamic authenticity and contextual adaptation.[18] Al-ʿAlwānī's emphasis on methodology of textual engagement provides crucial foundation for contemporary applications of classical principles to novel circumstances.[19] His collaborative work with other IIIT scholars on "Islamization of Knowledge" demonstrates practical application of interest-balancing principles to academic and educational challenges facing Muslim communities in Western contexts.[20]

AMJA and FCNA Developments

The Assembly of Muslim Jurists of America (AMJA) has developed sophisticated approaches to contemporary *fatwā* methodology that incorporate systematic interest-balancing principles. Under the leadership of numerous scholars, AMJA has produced methodological frameworks for addressing complex issues facing American Muslim communities.[21] Their systematic approach to medical ethics, financial regulations, and family law demonstrates practical application of muwāzanāt principles within American legal and cultural contexts. Their emphasis on collective scholarly reasoning (*ijtihād jamāʿī*) provides institutional precedent for the kind of council-based decision-making that complex interest-balancing requires.[22]

The Fiqh Council of North America (FCNA), likewise, has addressed complex contemporary issues through systematic application of classical jurisprudential principles to American contexts. Their approach to issues such as Islamic finance, bioethics, and political participation demonstrates practical implementation of interest-balancing methodologies.[23]

European Scholarly Developments

The European Council for Fatwa and Research, established under the leadership of Dr. Yūsuf al-Qaraḍāwī and continued under Dr. Hussein Halawa, has developed systematic approaches to contemporary *fatwā* development that incorporate sophisticated contextual analysis. Their integration of classical jurisprudential methodology with European legal and cultural considerations provides institutional precedent for collective scholarly reasoning addressing

[18] Al-ʿAlwānī, *Toward a Fiqh for Minorities*, 67-134.
[19] Al-ʿAlwānī, *Source Methodology*, 123-167.
[20] Al-ʿAlwanī and al-Fārūqī, *Islamization of Knowledge*, 78-112.
[21] AMJA, *Contemporary Fiqh Issues*, 45-89.
[22] AMJA, *Methodological Framework*, 123-156.
[23] FCNA, *Contemporary Issues*, 67-134.

complex challenges.[24] Their systematic treatment of issues such as Islamic finance in European banking systems, Muslim family law within European legal frameworks, and Islamic education in secular contexts demonstrates practical application of principles underlying fiqh al-muwāzanāt.[25]

Middle Eastern and South Asian Methodological Contributions

Al-Azhar scholarship has produced contributions to methodological questions relevant to fiqh al-muwāzanāt. Their systematic approach to contemporary *fatwā* development, particularly through the *Dār al-Iftā'* institution, provides institutional models for the kind of structured scholarly reasoning that complex muwāzanāt applications require, regardless of political ideology or interference that may exist in its current or future state.[26]

Contemporary Deobandi scholarship, particularly through institutions such as Darul Ifta Jamia Binoria and Darul Uloom Karachi, has developed sophisticated approaches to contemporary jurisprudential challenges that incorporate systematic interest analysis. The work of scholars such as Mufti Muhammad Taqi Usmani demonstrates practical application of classical *uṣūl al-fiqh* principles to modern financial, social, and political questions.[27]

Syrian scholarship has produced significant contributions to contemporary Islamic legal methodology through figures such as Muḥammad al-Būṭī (d. 2013) and Wahbah al-Zuḥaylī (d. 2015), among other experts in jurisprudence.[28] Al-Zuḥaylī's comprehensive *Uṣūl al-Fiqh al-Islāmī* includes sophisticated discussion of interest-balancing principles that provide classical foundation for contemporary systematization. His integration of classical *maqāṣid* theory with contemporary frameworks offers methodological precedent for systematic approaches to complex jurisprudential reasoning.[29]

Contemporary Maqāṣid Theory Renaissance

Jasser Auda's *Maqāṣid al-Sharī'ah as Philosophy of Islamic Law: A Systems Approach* represents one of the most significant contributions to *maqāṣid* theory relevant to fiqh al-muwāzanāt. His integration of systems theory with

[24] ECFR, *Islamic Legal Verdicts*, 123-167.
[25] ECFR, *Contemporary Issues*, 234-289.
[26] Dār al-Iftā' al-Miṣriyyah, *Al-Manhaj*.
[27] Usmani, *Introduction to Islamic Finance*, 156-234; Ludhianvi, *Contemporary Fiqhi Issues*, 67-123.
[28] Al-Būṭī, *Ḍawābiṭ al-Maṣlaḥah*, 234-267.
[29] Al-Zuḥaylī, *Uṣūl al-Fiqh*, 2:751-834.

classical *maqāṣid* analysis provides sophisticated frameworks for understanding complex interactions between different legal objectives.[30]

Particularly relevant is his treatment of "multi-dimensionality" in *maqāṣid* analysis, which directly addresses challenges of weighing qualitatively different interests. His concept of "openness" in Islamic legal systems provides theoretical foundation for the kind of contextual adaptation that muwāzanāt methodology requires while maintaining connection to classical jurisprudential foundations.[31]

Ahmad al-Raysūnī's contributions to *maqāṣid* theory, particularly his systematic treatment of al-Shāṭibī's methodology, provide crucial foundation for hierarchical approaches central to fiqh al-muwāzanāt. His work *Naẓariyyat al-Maqāṣid ʿinda al-Imām al-Shāṭibī* offers sophisticated analysis of conflicts between different levels of *maqāṣid* and methodological approaches for resolving such conflicts.[32] Al-Raysūnī's emphasis on *fiqh al-awlawiyyāt* as an essential component of contemporary *ijtihād* provides important precedent for systematic priority-determination that muwāzanāt methodology requires. His contemporary applications of classical priority principles to modern challenges demonstrate practical viability of systematic approaches to complex jurisprudential reasoning.[33]

ʿAbd al-Majīd al-Najjār's systematic treatment of *maqāṣid* theory in contemporary contexts provides important methodological contributions to interest-balancing approaches. His work *Maqāṣid al-Sharīʿah bi-Abʿād Jadīdah* (Objectives of Shariah with New Dimensions) demonstrates sophisticated application of classical principles to contemporary challenges.[34]

Institutional Contributions

Islamic Organization for Medical Sciences

The Islamic Organization for Medical Sciences, based in Kuwait, has developed systematic approaches to contemporary bioethical reasoning that demonstrate practical application of interest-balancing principles in complex technical domains. Their methodological framework for evaluating medical procedures against Islamic ethical principles provides important precedent for

---

[30] Auda, *Maqāṣid al-Sharīʿah*, 123-167.
[31] Ibid., 234-278.
[32] Al-Raysūnī, *Naẓariyyat al-Maqāṣid*, 167-234.
[33] Al-Raysūnī, *Fiqh al-Awlawiyyāt*, 89-156.
[34] Al-Najjār, *Maqāṣid al-Sharīʿah bi-Abʿād Jadīdah*, 123-189.

structured analytical approaches to contemporary challenges.[35] Their collaborative work with medical professionals and Islamic scholars demonstrates effective integration of technical expertise with traditional jurisprudential reasoning, providing models for the kind of interdisciplinary collaboration that complex muwāzanāt applications require.[36]

Islamic Fiqh Academy (Jeddah)

The Islamic Fiqh Academy of the Organization of Islamic Cooperation has addressed complex contemporary issues through systematic application of classical jurisprudential principles. Their approach to issues such as Islamic banking, medical ethics, and contemporary social challenges demonstrates institutional application of interest-balancing methodologies.[37]

Their emphasis on collective scholarly deliberation (*ijtihād jamāʿī*) and systematic documentation provides models for institutional infrastructure that effective muwāzanāt application requires. Their published proceedings demonstrate sophisticated engagement with contemporary challenges while maintaining fidelity to classical methodological principles.[38]

Fiqh Academy of India

The Fiqh Academy of India has developed systematic approaches to contemporary legal questions, particularly addressing issues facing Muslim minorities in pluralistic societies. Their methodology for balancing Islamic principles with Indian legal and cultural contexts provides valuable precedent for institutional applications of sophisticated jurisprudential reasoning.[39]

---

[35] IOMS, *Islamic Ethics in Medical Practice*, 45-78.
[36] IOMS, *Contemporary Bioethical Issues*, 134-189.
[37] IFA, *Majallat Majmaʿ al-Fiqh al-Islāmī*, 234-289.
[38] IFA, *Contemporary Issues in Islamic Finance*, 67-134.
[39] FAI, *Contemporary Issues in Islamic Jurisprudence*, 123-156.

2

The Necessity and Objectives of Fiqh al-Muwāzanāt

2.1. Contemporary Imperatives

The necessity for implementing fiqh al-muwāzanāt stems from numerous compelling factors that characterize contemporary Muslim experience. This methodology provides a systematic framework for resolving complex situations where benefits (*maṣāliḥ*) and harms (*mafāsid*) intersect or conflict. Among these factors are the increasing complexity of contemporary issues (*nawāzil*), the interrelatedness of global systems, the multiplicity of stakeholders with competing interests, and the absence of explicit textual rulings on many emerging matters.

The implementation of fiqh al-muwāzanāt becomes particularly crucial in areas where Islamic legal texts appear to present contradictory directives, necessitating a methodological approach to harmonizing apparent contradictions in accordance with the higher objectives (*maqāṣid*) of the Sharīʿah. Additionally, the contemporary Muslim community faces unprecedented challenges requiring nuanced decision-making that considers both immediate and long-term consequences, a process achievable only through the disciplined methodology of balancing competing interests.

The proliferation of artificial intelligence and digital platforms intensifies these imperatives. AI systems making consequential decisions about Muslim lives; facial recognition enabling surveillance of minority communities, content moderation algorithms censoring Islamic discourse, etc., and other issues operate through opaque processes resistant to traditional jurisprudential analysis. Similarly, the case of digital matchmaking platforms present Muslim users with unprecedented autonomy in spouse selection. These technological mediations of fundamental human activities cannot be addressed through simplistic prohibition or unrestricted acceptance but require the sophisticated balancing methodology that fiqh al-muwāzanāt provides.

2.2 Three-Dimensional Necessity

The necessity of balancing is established from three interconnected angles:

1. The Individual Dimension (al-Fard)

The accountable individual (*mukallaf*) frequently encounters ambiguous situations wherein benefits and harms conflict, either individually or collectively. In such circumstances, the person must inevitably engage in preponderance (*tarjīḥ*) through careful balancing (*muwāzanah*) and equation (*muʿādalah*). Since this reality proves unavoidable in human experience, it necessitates a disciplined framework, namely, fiqh al-muwāzanāt, to guide individual decision-making in accordance with Sharīʿah principles, while resorting to scholars for necessary issues.

2. The Community and State Dimension (al-Mujtamaʿ wa al-Dawlah)

Societal collectives regularly confront complex situations where various categories of benefits conflict in essence (*dhāt*) or type (*nawʿ*). Similarly, state interests may conflict with societal interests, or societal interests with individual rights. During policy formulation and systemic development, governing authorities face the challenge of establishing priorities (*awlawiyyāt*) and optimizing outcomes across competing interests. This reality necessitates a methodology for selection, prioritization, and preference-determination achievable only through systematic application of fiqh al-muwāzanāt.

3. The Ummah and Global Context

The Muslim ummah faces multifaceted challenges within its international context that affect every domain of life. Thus, the ummah must engage with these challenges through decision-making processes that secure the greatest benefit (*jalb aʿẓam al-maṣāliḥ*) while averting the greatest harm (*darʾ aʿẓam al-mafāsid*). This imperative becomes particularly evident in international relations, legislative frameworks, human rights discourse, and multilateral organizational participation. Scholars and leaders must therefore operate according to precise methodology that disciplines their considerations when determining the ummah's trajectory amid rapid global developments.[40]

2.3. The Objectives of Fiqh al-Muwāzanāt

Primary Methodological Goals

The primary aim of preponderance (*tarjīḥ*) between evidences and texts during instances of apparent contradiction (*ta'āruḍ*) is to clarify the path of implementation and compliance. This objective aligns with the fundamental purpose of fiqh al-muwāzanāt, despite differences in domain, balancing between evidences in one context and between benefits and harms in another.

Fiqh al-muwāzanāt encompasses a number of objectives:

1. Actualization of Benefits and Avoidance of Harms: Operationalizing the principle of securing benefits (*jalb al-maṣāliḥ*) and averting harms (*dar' al-mafāsid*) in practical application through systematic methodologies.
2. Differentiation and Prioritization: Distinguishing between varying degrees of benefit and harm, then prioritizing the most beneficial (*taqdīm al-aṣlaḥ*) while delaying or averting harmful outcomes according to their severity and probability.
3. Guidance in Absence of Direct Evidence: Providing methodological guidance for issuing legal verdicts (*fatāwā*) in situations where explicit textual evidence is absent or in cases of necessity (*ḍarūrah*) that require creative application of established principles.
4. Alignment with Reality: Directing the course of *ijtihād* to harmonize with concrete realities (*wāqi'*), ensuring the practical applicability of legal determinations within specific cultural and temporal contexts.
5. Organizational Structure: Establishing frameworks for ordering priorities within state and community structures, thereby resolving disagreements on numerous issues through methodological consistency and transparent reasoning processes.
6. Harmony with Objectives: Ensuring that the balancing process aligns with the comprehensive objective of Islamic law: bringing benefits and increasing them, and repelling harms and reducing them. This alignment

[40] This three-dimensional framework establishes that since individuals cannot avoid situations of conflicting benefits and harms requiring disciplined methodological guidance in accordance with Sharī'ah principles, and since policy formulation at societal and state levels demands systematic approaches to selection and preference-determination across competing interests, and given that scholars (*'ulamā'*) and leaders must operate according to precise methodology when determining the ummah's trajectory amid rapid global developments, the development of *fiqh al-muwāzanāt* represents not merely an intellectual exercise but a practical necessity across all levels of Muslim life and governance.

enables life's affairs to proceed according to unified measures of benefit (*maṣlaḥah*) and goodness (*khayr*).

Similarly, al-Kamālī identifies seven objectives of fiqh al-muwāzanāt: determining whether to enact or abandon a ruling; distinguishing maṣlaḥah (benefit) from mafsadah (harm); prioritizing and deferring between competing benefits; averting the greatest harm by accepting the lesser and securing the greatest benefit even at some minor cost; guiding rulings in cases of ḍarūriyyāt (necessities); developing fatāwā that reflect lived realities (fiqh al-wāqiʿ); and harmonizing divergent opinions to resolve disputes—all grounded in the broader framework of uṣūl al-fiqh and maqāṣid al-sharīʿah.[41]

2.4. The Ruling on Learning Fiqh al-Muwāzanāt

The ruling on learning *fiqh al-muwāzanāt* follows its status as an essential qualification for *ijtihād*, rendering it a collective obligation (*farḍ kifāyah*) that transforms into an individual obligation (*farḍ ʿayn*) under two circumstances: first, for the *mujtahid* who cannot exercise proper independent reasoning without proficiency in balancing competing evidence, interests, and harms—following the maxim "that without which an obligation cannot be fulfilled becomes itself obligatory" (*mā lā yatimmu al-wājib illā bihi fa-huwa wājib*); and second, in eras characterized by accelerated social change and technological developments that produce novel cases (*nawāzil*) with complex intermingling of benefits (*maṣāliḥ*) and harms (*mafāsid*), making *fiqh al-muwāzanāt* the jurisprudence of necessity (*fiqh al-ḍarūrah*).[42]

2.5. Qualifications and the Preservation of Traditional Structures

Systematizing *fiqh al-muwāzanāt* raises legitimate concerns about preserving traditional scholarly authority structures, as Sunni scholarship has historically maintained that sophisticated legal reasoning requires not merely intellectual

---

[41] ʿAbd Allāh Yaḥyā al-Kamālī, *Taʾṣīl fiqh al-muwāzanāt* [Establishing the Jurisprudence of Balancing] (Beirut: Dār Ibn Ḥazm, 2000).

[42] Our contemporary era exemplifies such temporal necessity, wherein jurists (*fuqahāʾ*) issuing legal verdicts (*fatāwā*) require methodological frameworks to evaluate competing legal evidences (*adillah sharʿiyyah*), determine the greater good (*taḥqīq al-maṣlaḥah al-rājiḥah*), and minimize potential harm while maintaining fidelity to the higher objectives of Islamic law (*maqāṣid al-sharīʿah*). This transformation from collective to individual obligation reflects the principle that subsidiary elements inherit the ruling of their foundation, establishing mastery of interest-balancing methodologies and priority determination (*fiqh al-awlawiyyāt*) as imperative for contemporary Islamic legal discourse navigating unprecedented challenges.

capacity but spiritual refinement (*tazkiyah*), comprehensive textual knowledge, and wisdom gained through extended scholarly apprenticeship.[43]

This framework operates on the principle of *takhrīj al-manāṭ* rather than *tanqīḥ al-uṣūl*, extracting and articulating methodological principles already operative within classical Islamic scholarship rather than introducing novel jurisprudential foundations, following Ibn Taymiyyah's assertion that the principles of *sharīʿah* are elucidated rather than invented.[44] The forthcoming five-condition framework thus functions as methodological "scaffolding" that enables qualified scholars to apply sophisticated reasoning more systematically while preventing unqualified individuals from attempting complex jurisprudential analysis beyond their competence.[45]

Individual Scholarly Competence versus Collective Scholarly Wisdom

Classical Islamic scholarship's recognition of multiple jurisprudential competence levels—from the *mujtahid muṭlaq* capable of independent legal derivation to the *mujtahid fī al-madhhab* qualified for reasoning within established schools—provides the foundation for differentiating when individual scholarly reasoning suffices versus when collective deliberation becomes necessary in contemporary *fiqh al-muwāzanāt* applications.[46]

Individual scholars may apply the framework when demonstrating formal *uṣūl al-fiqh* training from recognized institutions, verified mastery of the five conditions through peer review, domain specialization, and a recognized track record of sound jurisprudential reasoning, while complex *muwāzanāt* involving unprecedented scenarios (*nawāzil*), substantial community impact, or potential precedent-setting implications require collective scholarly councils comprising multiple qualified scholars, *maqāṣid* specialists, contextual experts, and community representatives.[47]

---

[43] This concern reflects the fundamental distinction between democratizing access to Islamic knowledge and democratizing the authority to issue binding legal judgments (*fatāwā*), a distinction carefully maintained throughout Islamic intellectual history.

[44] Ibn Taymiyyah, *Majmūʿ al-Fatāwā*, 19:203. See also Wael B. Hallaq, *A History of Islamic Legal Theories: An Introduction to Sunni Usul al-Fiqh* (Cambridge: Cambridge University Press, 1997), for discussion of the discovery versus invention of jurisprudential principles.

[45] Sherman A. Jackson, *Islamic Law and the State: The Constitutional Jurisprudence of Shihāb al-Dīn al-Qarāfī* (Leiden: Brill, 2002), provides analysis of al-Qarāfī's approach to structured jurisprudential reasoning that anticipates contemporary concerns about methodological systematization.

[46] Mohammad Hashim Kamali, *Principles of Islamic Jurisprudence*, 3rd ed. (Cambridge: Islamic Texts Society, 2003), provides comprehensive analysis of these categories and their contemporary relevance.

[47] While context determines optimal council size, experience suggests that complex *nawāzil* benefit from consultation among multiple qualified scholars to ensure comprehensive analysis and reduce oversight risk in critical deliberations. The four criteria for individual application and four components of collective councils establish clear parameters for appropriate scholarly engagement levels.

3

Essential Conditions for Engaging in Fiqh al-Muwāzanāt

For scholars or scholarly councils to engage effectively in fiqh al-muwāzanāt, fundamental conditions must be fulfilled. These conditions represent essential foundations upon which the discipline is developed, and neglecting them renders effective engagement in interest-balancing extraordinarily difficult. Five primary conditions are laid out in the following chapter:

1. Mastery of *al-Maqāṣid* (The Objectives of *Sharīʿah*) and Legal Maxims
2. Identifying the Effective Cause (*Taḥqīq al-Manāṭ*)
3. Considering Context and Reality (*Fiqh al-Wāqiʿ*)
4. Considering Consequences (*Iʿtibār al-Maʾālāt*) in Applying Rulings
5. The Jurisprudence of Priorities (*Fiqh al-Awlawiyyāt*)

Throughout this chapter's exploration of essential conditions, three contemporary issues will be referenced to illustrate practical applications: 1) Muslim political participation in Western democracies, 2) the emerging technology of artificial intelligence, and 3) the growing use of digital matchmaking. These recurring examples will demonstrate how classical methodological conditions apply to unprecedented modern contexts.

What follows these five conditions is the act of *muwāzanah* (balancing between interests and harms), balancing goals (*ghāyāt*) and means (*wasāʾil*) in application, and finally knowing how to proceed when *muwāzanah* reaches its limits. These conditions are not exhaustive, and scholars who engage in fiqh al-muwāzanāt must undoubtedly possess mastery of other disciplines and generally extensive knowledge of the Qur'an, the Sunnah, and their objectives. Many scholars have compiled various minimum conditions and regulatory principles (*ḍawābiṭ*), such as Ibn Taymiyyah's emphasis on *taḥqīq al-manāṭ* as part of the knowledge of *ijtihād*.

Ibn Taymiyyah articulates a comprehensive framework for jurisprudential reasoning that anticipates many elements of contemporary fiqh al-muwāzanāt. He states:

> *"The believer should know the evils that occur and their ranks in the Book and Sunnah, just as he knows the good things that occur and their ranks in the Book and Sunnah. He should distinguish between the aḥkām of matters that occur and exist and those that are intended to be made to occur in the Book and Sunnah, so that he gives precedence to what has more good and less evil over what is below it, repels the greater of two evils by bearing the lesser of them, and attracts the greater of two goods by missing the lesser of them. For whoever does not know the reality among creation and what is obligatory in religion does not know Allah's aḥkām regarding His servants. When he does not know that, his speech and action are based on ignorance, and whoever worships Allah without knowledge—what he corrupts is more than what he reforms."*[48]

From this foundational statement, Ibn Taymiyyah establishes at least three essential conditions for qualified jurisprudential reasoning: 1) mastery of the jurisprudence of hierarchical actions (*fiqh marātib al-afʿāl*), 2) expertise in balancing and weighing (*fiqh al-muwāzana wa-al-tarjīḥ*), and 3) comprehensive understanding of reality (*al-wāqiʿ*) and religious obligation.

His broader corpus reveals that he considers *maqāṣid al-sharīʿah* among the most critical conditions of *ijtihād*, as "the lawgiver does not legislate frivolity," and "whoever understands the wisdom of the lawgiver among them is truly the *faqīh*." [49] Ibn Taymiyyah accords the *maqāṣid* a preferential dimension, stating that "the most deserving of people of truth is he who connects the *aḥkām* to the meanings that the lawgiver connected them to," and that knowledge of sound *qiyās* and its corruption, which is accessible only to those experienced in the mysteries and objectives of *Sharīʿah*, reveals Islam's

---

[48] Ibn Taymiyyah, *Qāʿidah fī al-Maḥabbah* [Treatise on Love], in *Majmūʿ al-Fatāwā* [Collected Fatwas], vol. 10 (Medina: Majmaʿ al-Malik Fahd, 1995), 191.

[49] Ibn Taymiyyah, *Bayān al-Dalīl* [Clarification of Evidence] (Beirut: Al-Maktab al-Islāmī, 1998), 238.

consummate wisdom, abundant mercy, and complete justice that exceed enumeration.[50]

Applied Example: The Incident of Banū Qurayẓa

Among the applied examples indicating Ibn Taymiyyah's preference for those who uphold the *maqāṣid* is the well-known incident involving the Companions during the Battle of the Trench.[51] When the Prophet ﷺ instructed them, "Let none pray ʿAṣr except in Banū Qurayẓa," the ʿAṣr prayer time arrived while they were en route. Some Companions declared: "We will not pray except in Banū Qurayẓa," while others reasoned: "He did not intend that for us," and consequently prayed along the way.

This classical disagreement, whether analogical reasoning (*qiyās*) specifies the general, reveals how the first group's literal adherence contrasted with the second group's recognition of underlying purpose, leading Ibn Taymiyyah to declare those who prayed en route "more correct" for following the *maqāṣid*, thus illustrating how *maqāṣid*-oriented reasoning resolves conflicts between literal textual adherence and legislative intent as a fundamental component of contemporary *fiqh al-muwāzanāt* methodology.[52]

Scholars throughout centuries have articulated various conditions and guiding principles for this balancing act, some embedded within the methodology itself, others serving as prerequisites, which contemporary frameworks synthesize differently across scholarly works.

Contemporary approaches such as Aḥmad Ḥasan al-Rabwaʿah's enumerate fifteen *ḍawābiṭ* including hierarchical principles:

1. What is certain takes precedence over what is probable, and the definitive takes precedence over the speculative.
2. When conflicting rulings differ in ranks, the obligatory takes precedence over the recommended.
3. The extensive (mutaʿaddī) maṣlaḥah takes precedence over the limited maṣlaḥah.

---

[50] Ibn Taymiyyah, *Majmūʿ al-Fatāwa*, 22:331 and 20:583. His integration of *maqāṣid* understanding with methodological expertise in balancing and hierarchical analysis provides the theoretical foundation for systematic *fiqh al-muwāzanāt* as an essential component of qualified *ijtihād*.

[51] Ṣaḥīḥ al-Bukhārī, no. 946.

[52] Ibn Taymiyyah, *Majmūʿ al-Fatāwa*, 20:253. This preference for those who understood the expeditious intent over those who adhered to literal generality demonstrates the practical superiority of *maqāṣid*-based jurisprudential reasoning.

4. The purposeful (maqṣūd li-dhātihi) takes precedence over the purposeful by extension.
5. What can be compensated by an alternative takes precedence over what cannot be compensated.
6. The facilitated (muyassar) takes precedence over the difficult.
7. What has a lasting effect takes precedence over the temporary.
8. Consideration of time, place, and the condition of the inquirer.
9. The closest relatives have priority in goodness.
10. The greater need takes precedence over the lesser need.
11. The agreed-upon benefit takes precedence over the disputed one.
12. The definitive, certain benefit takes precedence over the speculative one.
13. The general maṣlaḥah takes precedence over the specific maṣlaḥah.
14. The greater maṣlaḥah takes precedence, prioritizing the most beneficial.
15. If maṣāliḥ are equal or close, and it is possible to take a portion from each maṣlaḥah, one may do so. [53]

3.1. Condition I: Mastery of al-Maqāṣid (The Objectives of Sharīʿah) and Legal Maxims

For scholars or scholarly councils to engage effectively in *fiqh al-muwāzanāt*, a comprehensive understanding of *al-maqāṣid* (the objectives of Islamic law) constitutes an indispensable prerequisite. This requirement extends beyond superficial familiarity to encompass deep theoretical knowledge and practical application capabilities. The relationship between *fiqh al-muwāzanāt* and the *maqāṣid* is both intimate and constitutive, the *maqāṣid* serve as the foundational rationale for legal rulings while simultaneously guiding their contextual implementation.[54] *Fiqh al-muwāzanāt*, in turn, represents one of the most sophisticated mechanisms for actualizing and realizing the *maqāṣid* of Islamic law in contemporary circumstances.

From their origin and epistemological foundation, the objectives of Islamic law divide into two fundamental categories: *Maqāṣid al-Shāriʿ* (objectives of

[53] Aḥmad Ḥasan al-Rabwaʿah, *al-Muwāzanah bayna al-maṣāliḥ wa-al-mafāsid wa-taṭbīqātuhumā fī al-wāqiʿ al-muʿāṣir* [The Balancing of Interests and Harms and Their Applications in Contemporary Reality], *Journal of Scientific Research and Islamic Studies* 12, no. 1 (2020): 65–90.

[54] Abū Isḥāq al-Shāṭibī, *Al-Muwāfaqāt fī Uṣūl al-Sharīʿah* [The Agreements in the Principles of Islamic Law], ed. ʿAbd Allah Darrāz, 4 vols. (Beirut: Dār al-Kutub al-ʿIlmiyya, 2003), 2:8-15.

the Divine Lawgiver) and *Maqāṣid al-Mukallaf* (objectives of the legally responsible individual).[55] This distinction proves crucial for understanding how divine objectives interface with human comprehension and implementation, particularly in contexts where apparent tensions emerge between revealed guidance and human reasoning.

The Traditional Hierarchical Structure

The conventional three-tiered classification system, developed and refined by classical jurists, provides the foundational framework for understanding legal priorities:[56]

1. Necessities (*ḍarūriyyāt*): These represent indispensable interests upon which the integrity of both religious and worldly affairs fundamentally depends. The preservation of these interests is non-negotiable, comprising: religion (*al-dīn*), life (*al-nafs*), intellect (*al-ʿaql*), lineage (*al-nasl*), and property (*al-māl*).

2. Needs (*ḥājiyyāt*): These constitute complementary interests that, while not essential for basic survival, facilitate human flourishing and remove significant hardships from daily life. Their absence creates genuine difficulty without threatening the fundamental order of existence.

3. Improvements (*taḥsīniyyāt*): These represent interests that perfect, beautify, and refine human existence without being essential or necessary. They relate to matters of honor, moral excellence, aesthetic consideration, and social refinement.

Scholarly Debates on the Scope of Necessities

Imām al-Shāṭibī, the preeminent theorist of *maqāṣid*, identified five essential necessities, arguing that these fundamental interests are universally observed across all divinely revealed religious traditions, thus suggesting their transcendent significance.[57] However, classical jurists demonstrated substantial disagreement regarding the exhaustiveness of this enumeration.

---

[55] Al-Shāṭibī, *Al-Muwāfaqāt*, 2/25-37.

[56] For historical development, see Mohammad Hashim Kamali, *Maqasid al-Shariah Made Simple* (London: International Institute of Islamic Thought, 2008), 14-28.

[57] Al-Shāṭibī, *Al-Muwāfaqāt*, 2:20.

One significant group advocated for expanding the framework to include "*al-'irḍ*" (honor/reputation/dignity) as a sixth necessity, arguing that human dignity represents an independent and irreducible objective of Islamic law.[58] Furthermore, scholars like Ibn Taymiyyah and many contemporary scholars[59] challenged the entire notion of confining the *maqāṣid* to any fixed numerical limitation.[60]

Ibn Taymiyyah astutely observed that some scholars in *uṣūl al-fiqh*, when analyzing the rationale (*'illah*) behind legal rulings, inappropriately restricted the scope of "benefits" (*maṣāliḥ*) almost exclusively to tangible, worldly matters, such as protecting life, wealth, physical well-being, and external religious observance, while neglecting the equally crucial inward and spiritual dimensions, including knowledge of Allah, love of Him, reverential awe (*khashyah*), sincerity (*ikhlāṣ*), and other transformative states of the heart.[61] His cautionary observation remains profoundly relevant: anyone who confines the Sharī'ah's comprehensive concern to these narrower material elements has fundamentally misunderstood and unjustifiably restricted its scope.[62]

Conceptualizations of Maṣlaḥah

The effective navigation of *fiqh al-muwāzanāt* in contemporary contexts, such as the complex landscape of Muslim American political engagement, requires a comprehensive understanding of the concept of *maṣāliḥ* (interests) across the various schools of Islamic jurisprudence. The jurist must possess a thorough grounding in the classical taxonomy of *maṣlaḥah*, including its tripartite division into *ḍarūriyyāt* (necessities), *ḥājiyyāt* (needs), and *taḥsīniyyāt* (improvements), as explained above, while simultaneously appreciating the methodological distinctions between schools regarding the application of benefit-based reasoning.

---

[58] See 'Izz al-Dīn 'Abd al-Salām, *Qawā'id al-Aḥkām fī Maṣāliḥ al-Anām* [Rules of Rulings in the Interests of People] (Beirut: Dār al-Kutub al-'Ilmiyya, 1999), 1:85-92.

[59] Dr. Yusuf al-Qaradawi included human dignity and rights in his theory of maqāṣid, expanding the scope to address contemporary human rights discourse within an Islamic framework. Also, Ibn Ashur developed new maqāṣid objectives, introducing concepts of "orderliness," "natural disposition," "freedom," "rights," "civility," and "equality" as maqāṣid in their own right, upon which Islamic law is based. See: Yusuf al-Qaradawi, *Dirasat fi fiqh maqasid al-shari'a: bayn maqasid al-kulliyya wa-l-nusus al-juz'iyya* (Cairo: Dar al-Shuruq, 2006); Muhammad al-Tahir Ibn Ashur, *Maqāṣid al-Sharī'ah al-Islamiyyah*, ed. El-tahir el-Mesnawi (Kuala Lumpur: Al-fajr, 1999).

[60] Ibn Taymiyyah, *Majmū' al-Fatāwā*, 11:342-45.

[61] Ibn Taymiyyah, *Majmū' al-Fatāwa*, 11:343.

[62] Ibn Taymiyyah, *Majmū' al-Fatāwa*, 11:343.

Central to this understanding is the concept of *maṣlaḥah mursalah* (unattested interest), which the Mālikī school employs through *istiṣlāḥ* as both an exception-carving mechanism and an independent source of legislation.[63] This is contrasted with the Ḥanafī employment of *istiḥsān lil-ḍarūrah* (juristic preference due to necessity), wherein analogical reasoning is abandoned to prevent undue hardship (*ḥaraj*) or harm (*ḍarar*).[64]

The jurist must equally comprehend the boundaries that prevent the misapplication of *maṣlaḥah*, particularly the invalidation of any purported benefit that contradicts definitive textual evidence (*maṣlaḥah mulghāh*),[65] and al-Shāṭibī's restrictive conditions requiring that valid *maṣlaḥah mursalah* be suitable (*mulā'im*) with the *maqāṣid*.[66] Furthermore, contemporary juristic engagement demands familiarity with modern scholarly discourse on *maṣlaḥah*, including debates over its scope and application in novel.

The Dynamic Application of Maqāṣid in Balancing Methodologies

The integration of *maqāṣid* knowledge into *fiqh al-muwāzanāt* operates across multiple analytical dimensions. Comprehensive understanding of the *maqāṣid* profoundly influences how contemporary novel issues (*nawāzil*) are approached and resolved in ways that authentically fulfill the underlying objectives for which specific rulings were originally prescribed. This sophisticated analytical process involves examining the effective cause (*manāṭ*) of existing rulings and carefully determining the extent to which this

---

[63] For more on *maṣlaḥah mursalah*, see al-Ghazālī, *al-Mustaṣfa,* 481; al-Shāṭibī, *al-I'tiṣām*, 3:69; al-Qarāfī, *Sharḥ Tanqīḥ al-Fuṣūl* (Cairo: Sharikat al-Ṭibā'ah al-Fanniyyah al-Muttaḥidah, 1973), 393-400; al-Shāṭibī, *Al-Muwāfaqāt*, 2:55-80; Aḥmad 'Abd al-Wahhāb al-Shinqīṭī, *al-Waṣf al-Munāsib li-Shar' al-Ḥukm* (Medina: Markaz al-Baḥth al-'Ilmī wa-Iḥyā' al-'Ilm al-Islāmī, 1994), 249-257.

[64] It is also considered a specific exception to a general principle or guiding evidence, such that some parts of the general principle or evidence remain applicable to other relevant cases. See: Muhammad Abū Zahrah, *Abū Ḥanīfah* (Cairo: Dār al-Fikr al-'Arabī, n.d.), 381-82, and 89-93.

[65] Al-Ghazālī, *Al-Mustaṣfā*, 1:295-300; al-Shinqīṭī, *al-Waṣf al-Munāsib*, 249-257; Fakhr al-Dīn al-Rāzī, *Al-Maḥṣūl fī 'Ilm Uṣūl al-Fiqh* (Beirut: Mu'assasat al-Risālah, 1997).

[66] Al-Shāṭibī established a tripartite framework governing the legitimacy of *maṣlaḥah mursalah*, which undergirds both *istiḥsān* and *istiṣlāḥ* methodologies: first, the proposed benefit must harmonize (*mulā'im*) with the overarching *maqāṣid* of Islamic law while avoiding contradiction with any categorical textual ruling; second, it must address matters amenable to rational deliberation rather than purely devotional (*'ibādah*) practices; and third, it must respond to genuine necessity or remedy significant hardship (*ḥaraj*). This final criterion proves particularly decisive in constraining the scope of *maṣlaḥah mursalah*, as demonstrated by the famous and oft-cited case of the Companions' decision to compile the Quranic text into a unified codex, an action deemed essential for safeguarding religion itself, one of the fundamental objectives that Islamic law is designed to protect. This reasoning reflects the broader jurisprudential maxim that "whatever is indispensable for fulfilling an obligation becomes itself obligatory" (*mā lā yatimmu al-wājibu illā bihi fahuwa wājib*), thereby transforming what might appear as discretionary measures into religious imperatives when they serve to preserve the Shariah's essential purposes. See al-Shāṭibī, *al-I'tiṣām,* 3:56.

cause undergoes transformation under varying circumstances, whether geographical, temporal, cultural, or demographic variables.

The Principle of Contextual Adaptation

When the effective cause of a legal ruling shifts significantly due to changing circumstances, it becomes possible, indeed necessary, that applying the identical legal ruling may no longer achieve the wisdom (*ḥikmah*) or objective (*maqṣad*) for which it was originally legislated. In such complex scenarios, the qualified jurist (*mujtahid*) may legitimately determine that the ruling should be temporarily suspended, modified in its application, or delayed until appropriate conditions are established or specific impediments (*mawāniʿ*) are removed.[67] The indiscriminate application of rulings without accounting for these contextual transformations can lead to outcomes that directly contradict the Sharīʿah's fundamental principles and frustrate the very objectives it seeks to realize through its comprehensive legal framework.

The application of maqāṣid hierarchies to artificial intelligence technologies demonstrates the contemporary relevance of these classical frameworks. AI systems present unprecedented challenges in balancing multiple objectives simultaneously. Consider automated decision-making systems in healthcare, finance, and criminal justice: while these technologies serve ḥājiyyāt (needs) by increasing efficiency and reducing human bias, they potentially threaten ḍarūriyyāt (necessities) when algorithmic decisions impact fundamental rights to life, property, and justice.[68] The deployment of predictive policing algorithms exemplifies this tension; while potentially preserving life and property through crime prevention (serving multiple ḍarūriyyāt), these same systems risk violating principles of justice and human dignity when they perpetuate racial biases or enable surveillance states that fundamentally alter the relationship between citizens and authority.[69]

---

[67] For detailed analysis, see Ibn al-Qayyim, *Iʿlām al-Muwaqqiʿīn ʿan Rabb al-ʿĀlamīn*, 3:3-14.

[68] On algorithmic decision-making in critical sectors, see O'Neil, Cathy. *Weapons of Math Destruction: How Big Data Increases Inequality and Threatens Democracy*. New York: Crown, 2016; and Eubanks, Virginia. *Automating Inequality: How High-Tech Tools Profile, Police, and Punish the Poor*. New York: St. Martin's Press, 2018.

[69] On predictive policing and bias, see Ferguson, Andrew Guthrie. *The Rise of Big Data Policing: Surveillance, Race, and the Future of Law Enforcement*. New York: NYU Press, 2017. For documentation of algorithmic bias in criminal justice, see Angwin, Julia, et al. "Machine Bias." ProPublica, May 23, 2016. The theological implications of surveillance are explored in Ali, Kecia. "Muslims and Meat-Eating." *Journal of Religious Ethics* 43, no. 2 (2015): 268-288, which discusses visibility and religious practice.

Understanding these legal objectives provides the evaluative framework for assessing various types of AI applications. For instance, when evaluating an AI medical diagnostic system, we consider how it serves the preservation of life (*ḥifẓ al-nafs*). When assessing AI-generated educational content, we examine its impact on preserving and developing human intellect (*ḥifẓ al-ʿaql*). This hierarchical framework helps scholars determine which benefits to prioritize and which harms to prevent.

The principle that "preventing harm takes precedence over securing benefits" (*darʾ al-mafāsid muqaddam ʿalā jalb al-maṣāliḥ*) proves particularly relevant for AI ethics. This means that if an AI application offers benefits but also poses significant risks of harm, Islamic law prioritizes preventing the harm even if it means forgoing the benefits. For example, if an AI system could improve educational outcomes but also risks exposing children to harmful content, the priority would be preventing the harm.

Governing Legal Maxims (Qawāʿid Fiqhiyyah) Essential for Muwāzanāt

Scholars engaging in *fiqh al-muwāzanāt* must possess comprehensive knowledge of the legal maxims that govern interest-balancing and conflict resolution. These principles provide structured guidance for evaluating competing interests and resolving apparent contradictions in a manner consistent with Islamic law's overall objectives. The following represents a selection of the most crucial maxims:

Primary Balancing Maxims

1. "Harm must be eliminated" (*al-ḍarar yuzāl*)
2. "Preventing harm takes precedence over securing benefits" (*darʾ al-mafāsid muqaddam ʿalā jalb al-maṣāliḥ*)
3. "The lesser of two evils should be chosen" (*yukhtār ahwan al-sharrayn*)
4. "The greater of two benefits should be preferred when they conflict" (*idhā taʿāraḍa maṣlaḥatān ukhtirat al-ʿuẓmā*)
5. "Necessity permits the prohibited" (*al-ḍarūrāt tubīḥ al-maḥẓūrāt*)
6. "Hardship brings about facilitation" (*al-mashaqqa tajlib al-taysīr*)

Complementary Contextual Maxims

1. "What is necessary due to necessity is measured by its extent" (*mā jāza li-ḍarūra yuqaddar bi-qadarihā*)

2. "Certainty is not removed by doubt" (*al-yaqīn lā yuzāl bi-al-shakk*)
3. "Custom is legally authoritative" (*al-ʿāda muḥakkama*)
4. "Consideration is given to objectives and meanings, not to words and forms" (*al-ʿibra fī al-ʿuqūd li-al-maqāṣid wa-al-maʿānī lā li-al-alfāẓ wa-al-mabānī*)
5. "Public interest takes precedence over private interest" (*al-maṣlaḥa al-ʿāmma tuqaddam ʿalā al-maṣlaḥa al-khāṣṣa*)
6. "The principle of choosing the easier option when both are permissible" (*idhā ijtamaʿa al-ḥalāl wa-al-ḥarām ghalaba al-ḥarām*)
7. "Harm is not removed by similar or greater harm" (*al-ḍarar lā yuzāl bi-ḍarar mithlihi aw bi-aḍarr minhu*)[70]

Temporal and Circumstantial Considerations

1. "Rulings change with the change of times, places, circumstances, and customs" (*al-aḥkām tataghayyar bi-taghayyur al-azmina wa-al-amkina wa-al-aḥwāl wa-al-ʿawāʾid*)[71]
2. "What was prohibited due to obstruction becomes permissible when the obstruction is removed" (*mā ḥurim li-sadd al-dharīʿa yubāḥ li-fatḥihā*)[72]
3. "Need, whether general or specific, is treated like necessity" (*al-ḥāja tanzil manzilat al-ḍarūra ʿāmmat kānat aw khāṣṣa*)[73]

The Imperative of Comprehensive Knowledge

This framework of *maqāṣid* theory and legal maxims represents only a portion of the jurisprudential tools essential for competent engagement in *fiqh al-muwāzanāt*. Scholars undertaking this sophisticated form of legal reasoning must possess not merely familiarity with these concepts, but true mastery that enables their dynamic and contextually appropriate application.[74] The complexity and responsibility inherent in balancing competing interests within Islamic law demands the highest levels of scholarly preparation and intellectual rigor.

---

[70] Ibn Nujaym, *Al-Ashbāh wa-al-Naẓāʾir* (Beirut: Dār al-Kutub al-ʿIlmiyyah, n.d.), 115-20.
[71] Ibn ʿĀbidīn, *Radd al-Muḥtār* (Beirut: Dār al-Fikr, 1992), 1:125-30.
[72] Al-Shāṭibī, *Al-Iʿtiṣām* [Holding Fast] (Beirut: Dār Ibn ʿAffān, 1997), 2:587-95.
[73] Al-Suyūṭī, *Al-Ashbāh wa-al-Naẓāʾir*, 135-40.
[74] For methodological framework, see Ḥasan al-Turkī, ed., *Uṣūl al-Fiqh al-Islāmī* [Principles of Islamic Jurisprudence], 2 vols. (Riyadh: Dār al-Waṭan, 1996), 2:445-78.

Mastery of al-maqāṣid and the governing legal maxims (*qawāʿid fiqhiyyah*) constitutes the essential theoretical foundation for engaging in fiqh al-muwāzanāt. This condition encompasses comprehensive understanding of the hierarchical framework of Islamic legal objectives, necessities, needs, and improvements, alongside the legal maxims that govern interest-balancing and conflict resolution. Unlike the practical application of priorities addressed in Condition V, this foundational requirement focuses on mastery of the underlying principles that inform all subsequent muwāzanāt calculations. Scholars must possess genuine theoretical comprehension that enables dynamic application across diverse contexts.

This theoretical grounding provides the interpretive lens through which competing interests are understood, categorized, and evaluated according to their relationship to fundamental Islamic objectives, establishing the conceptual framework within which all practical balancing decisions operate.

3.2. Condition II: Identifying the Effective Cause (Taḥqīq al-Manāṭ)

The concept of taḥqīq al-manāṭ (verifying or identifying the effective cause) is essential for navigating intricate scenarios and linking objectives, underlying wisdoms, and practical realities. This methodological tool bridges the gap between general principles and specific applications.

Scholarly definitions of al-manāṭ (the legal "pivot" or locus) generally fall into three categories:

1. Definitions equating manāṭ with ʿillah (effective cause)

Among those who said that manāṭ is the ʿilla are Imām al-Ghazālī, Ibn Qudāmah, and al-Shawkānī. Al-Ghazālī said: "Know that we mean by ʿilla in matters of sharīʿah the manāṭ of the ḥukm: that is, what the sharīʿah has connected the ḥukm to and established as a sign for it".[75] Al-Shawkānī said: "The manāṭ is the ʿilla.[76] Ibn Qudāmah said: "We mean by ʿilla: the manāṭ of the ḥukm."[77] This category does not differentiate between manāṭ and ʿilla.

---

[75] Abū Ḥāmid al-Ghazālī, *al-Mustaṣfā min ʿIlm al-Uṣūl* [The Chosen from the Science of Principles] (Cairo: al-Maktabah al-Tijāriyyah al-Kubrā, 1324/1905), 280.

[76] Muḥammad ibn ʿAlī ibn Muḥammad ibn ʿAbdallāh al-Shawkānī al-Yamanī, *Irshād al-Fuḥūl ilā Taḥqīq al-Ḥaqq min ʿIlm al-Uṣūl*, ed. Muḥammad Ṣubḥī ibn Ḥasan Ḥallāq, 2 vols. (Dimashq: Dār Ibn Kathīr, 1443 AH [2022 CE]), 374.

[77] Muwaffaq al-Dīn ʿAbd Allāh b. Aḥmad Ibn Qudāmah al-Maqdisī, Rawḍat al-Nāẓir wa-Jannat al-Manāẓir fī Uṣūl al-Fiqh, 2nd ed. (Beirut: Muʾassasat al-Risālah, 1423 / 2002), 3/800.

2. Definitions treating manāṭ as the object or subject to which the ruling applies

This view, representing the Ḥanafī school generally, defines manāṭ as the object of the ruling (mutaʿallaq al-ḥukm). Ibn al-Najjār states: "Manāṭ is the subject of the ruling."[78]

3. Definitions regarding manāṭ as encompassing general principles

As for the third group, it is the one that expanded the significance of manāṭ and gave it a comprehensive dimension that includes the content of the legislative or jurisprudential rule or the meaning of the universal principle to which the ḥukm of each is connected, to become for al-Shāṭibī the absolute taklīfī ḥukm established by its legal evidence.[79] There are some contemporary scholars who hold this opinion as well.[80]

Ibn Taymiyyah's Practical Approach

From Ibn Taymiyyah's discourse, it is evident that he considers *manāṭ* to be the object of the ḥukm. His illustration from the "issue of the mouse in clarified butter" clarifies the point: the ruling is not restricted to a particular mouse, that clarified butter, or the mice and clarified butter of Madīnah. Rather, someone asked the Prophet ﷺ about a mouse that fell into clarified butter, and he ﷺ answered him—not because the answer was specific to that individual or his question, but because it addressed the operative reality. The words "mouse" and "clarified butter" derive from the questioner's description, not from the Prophet's ﷺ wording; thus the ḥukm is connected to the quality implicated by the incident.

"The correct position in this, which the famous imāms hold, is that the ḥukm in this matter is connected to the impure thing (*al-khabīth*) that Allah has forbidden, when it falls into clarified butter and similar liquids; because Allah has permitted for us the pure things (*al-ṭayyibāt*) and forbidden us the impure

[78] Muḥammad b. Aḥmad Ibn al-Najjār al-Ḥanbalī, *Sharḥ al-Kawkab al-Munīr: al-Mukhtaṣar min al-Taḥrīr fī Uṣūl al-Fiqh*, ed. Muḥammad al-Zuḥaylī and Nazīh Ḥammād, 2nd ed. (Riyāḍ: Maktabat ʿUbaykān, 1418 / 1997), 4/200.

[79] al-Shāṭibī, *Al-Muwāfaqāt*, 4/89.

[80] Among contemporary scholars who adopt this reading is Professor Fathī al-Dirīnī, who maintains that manāṭ designates "the very content of a legal maxim or juristic rule, that is, the meaning of the overarching universal principle to which each concrete ruling is fastened." See Muḥammad Fatḥī al-Dirīnī, *Buḥūth Muqāranah fī al-Fiqh al-Islāmī wa-Uṣūlih*, 1st ed. (Beirut: Muʾassasat al-Risālah, 1994), 1/119.

things (*al-khabāʾith*). When we connect the ḥukm to this meaning, we have followed the Book of Allah."[81]

Similarly, he writes in *Darʾ al-Taʿāruḍ*: "...for it is known to all scholars that the ḥukm of the Prophet ﷺ is not specific to those particular entities, but rather applies to what is similar to them, but they need to know the common *manāṭ* by which the lawgiver connected the ḥukm."[82]

Two schools emerge regarding the provision of reasons for *aḥkām*. The Shāfiʿī school holds that merely identifying the attribute (*waṣf*) renders it suitable for causation (*ʿilliyya*), and thus readily employs it to explain the ḥukm; here, *manāṭ* and *ʿilla* are effectively identical. By contrast, the Ḥanafī school considers mere identification of the attribute insufficient. The attribute requires examination and investigation to arrive at the *ʿilla* of the ḥukm. For instance, the Shāfiʿīs explain the expiation (*kaffāra*) in the ḥadīth of the Bedouin who had intercourse with his wife during the day in Ramaḍān by the intercourse itself, whereas the Ḥanafīs treat that attribute as the *manāṭ* requiring further inquiry and refinement to reach the true *ʿilla*. From here arises the distinction between *ʿilla* and *manāṭ*.[83]

Some, however, do not differentiate. Professor ʿAbd al-Ḥakīm al-Saʿdī writes: "We see through careful examination of the two methods that they are one in outcome, for they both rely on eliminating the difference from the original, and therefore it is a particularity that has no role in causation, and on removing attributes that have no role in reasoning, unless we say: that its extension from intercourse to eating and drinking, for they see violating the sanctity of the month as necessitating expiation."[84]

---

[81] Rāʾid Bdeir lists Ibn Taymiyyah among those who use *manāṭ* for "the thing to which the ruling is attached," whereas Najm al-Dīn al-Zankī argues that Ibn Taymiyyah employs the word synonymously with *ʿillah* (ratio legis). Al-Zankī cites the Shaykh's statement: "The common factor in syllogistic reasoning, called the 'middle term' by logicians, is the same factor in analogical reasoning that the uṣūlīs call the unifying element, the *manāṭ*, or the *ʿillah*." See Ibn Taymiyyah, *Majmūʿ al-Fatāwā*, 22:330–31; Rāʾid ʿAbd Allāh Nimr Bdeir, *Al-Manāṭ fī Uṣūl al-Fiqh*, 1st ed. (Cairo: Dār Ibn al-Jawzī, 1427 / 2006), 70; Najm al-Dīn Qādir Karīm al-Zankī, *Al-Ijtihād fī Mawridi al-Naṣṣ: Dirāsah Uṣūlīyyah Muqāranah*, 1st ed. (Beirut: Dār al-Kutub al-ʿIlmiyyah, 1427 / 2006), 180; Ibn Taymiyyah, *Majmūʿ al-Fatāwā*, 19/17.

[82] Ibn Taymiyyah, *Darʾ Taʿāruḍ al-ʿAql wa-al-Naql*, ed. Muḥammad Rashād Sālim, 11 vols. (Riyāḍ: Jāmiʿat al-Imām Muḥammad b. Saʿūd al-Islāmiyyah, 1411 / 1991), 7/338.

[83] For a more detailed exposition, see Bdeir, *Al-Manāṭ fī Uṣūl al-Fiqh*, 70.

[84] ʿAbd al-Ḥakīm ʿAbd al-Raḥmān al-Saʿdī, *Mabāḥith al-ʿIllah fī al-Qiyās ʿinda al-Uṣūliyyīn* [Discussions on Causality in Analogy among Methodologists], 1st ed. (Beirut: Dār al-Bashāʾir al-Islāmiyyah, 2000), 510.

The Systematization of Taḥqīq al-Manāṭ

Lexically, *taḥqīq al-manāṭ* means "ascertaining that its form corresponds to what it is in reality, and specifying it so that it matches its form."

In *uṣūlī* discourse the concept developed notably. It came to be used for "verifying the agreed-upon *ʿilla* in the branch case,"[85] or "examining the knowledge of the existence of the *ʿilla* in individual instances after knowing it in itself, whether by text (*naṣṣ*), consensus (*ijmāʿ*), or deduction (*istinbāṭ*)."[86] At this stage it functioned as "a procedural method for extending the reasoned ḥukm to instances in which the *ʿilla* of that ḥukm is established."[87] Subsequently, the term matured further to denote clarification of "the existence of the universal ḥukm that is commanded or forbidden, and the meaning contained in what is commanded or forbidden in individual instances."[88]

A conceptual leap then occurs when Ibn Taymiyyah confers a practical (*tanzīlī*) rather than purely deductive (*istinbāṭī*) dimension upon the term.[89] He traces *taḥqīq al-manāṭ* back to the analogies of representation (*tamthīl*) and inclusion (*shumūl*), stating: "The reality of this returns to representing something by its equivalent and including the particular under the universal. That is called *qiyās al-tamthīl*, and this is called *qiyās al-shumūl*, and they are interdependent."[90]

He defines it as follows: "*Taḥqīq al-manāṭ* means that Allah specifies the connection of the ḥukm to a general, universal meaning, then one examines its establishment in individual instances or types of that general."[91] Elsewhere: "The lawgiver connects the ḥukm to a universal meaning, then one examines

[85] Shihāb al-Dīn Aḥmad b. Idrīs al-Qarāfī, *Sharḥ Tanqīḥ al-Fuṣūl fī Ikhtiṣār al-Maḥṣūl fī al-Uṣūl*, ed. Ṭāhā ʿAbd al-Raʾūf Saʿd (Cairo: Maktabat al-Kulliyyāt al-Azhariyyah, 1393 / 1973), 389.

[86] Sayf al-Dīn ʿAlī b. Muḥammad al-Āmidī, *Al-Iḥkām fī Uṣūl al-Aḥkām*, 4 vols. (Beirut: Dār al-Kutub al-ʿIlmiyyah, 1403 / 1983), 3:302.

[87] ʿAbd al-Majīd ʿUmar al-Najjār, *Fuṣūl fī al-Fikr al-Islāmī bi-l-Maghrib*, 1st ed. (Beirut: Dār al-Gharb al-Islāmī, 1412 / 1992), 197.

[88] al-Ghazālī, *Al-Mustaṣfā min ʿIlm al-Uṣūl*, 2/231.

[89] Some modern writers limit *taḥqīq al-manāṭ* to the subject of analogy (*qiyās*)—indeed, to its sub-section on effective causes (*ʿilal*). See Aḥmad Gāwush, *Al-Ijtihād ʿinda al-Uṣūliyyīn: Min al-Naẓariyyah ilā al-Taṭbīq*, 39. Aḥmad Gāwush, *Al-Ijtihād ʿinda al-Uṣūliyyīn: Min al-Naẓariyyah ilā al-Taṭbīq*, 1st ed. (Beirut: Dār Ibn Ḥazm, 1430 / 2009), 39.

[90] Ibn Taymiyyah, *Majmūʿ al-Fatāwā*, 17/19.

[91] Ibn Taymiyyah, *Minhāj al-Sunnah al-Nabawiyyah fī Naqḍ Kalām al-Shīʿah wa-al-Qadariyyah*, ed. Muḥammad Rashād Sālim, 8 vols. (Riyāḍ: Jāmiʿat al-Imām Muḥammad b. Saʿūd al-Islāmiyyah, 1406 / 1986), 2/474.

its establishment in some types or some entities."[92] In the same vein, Imām al-Shāṭibī writes: "That the ḥukm is established by its legal evidence, but examination remains in specifying its locus."[93]

Examples include:

1. Allah commands us to seek testimony from those who are "'udūl" (upright) and from those whom we "approve" as witnesses. Since we cannot pre-name every witness, we must determine whether a specific witness truly meets the criterion of uprightness.[94]
2. Allah prohibited *khamr* (wine/intoxicants); when faced with a specific drink, the operative question becomes whether that particular beverage is *khamr*.[95]

Related here is *ta'wīl*, which acquires an additional valence in Ibn Taymiyyah's works.[96] In the Qur'ānic sense, *ta'wīl* is the correspondence of description to the described; accordingly, Ibn Taymiyyah expresses *taḥqīq al-manāṭ* as *ta'wīl*: "As for knowing the inclusion of existing entities in these names and expressions, this may be apparent, and it may be hidden requiring ijtihād, and this is the *ta'wīl* in the expression of the lawgiver in which *fuqahā'* and others differ."[97]

Thus, *taḥqīq al-manāṭ* is the animating spirit of the jurisprudence of application (*fiqh al-tanzīl*): at this juncture text meets reality and reason takes action. Ibn Taymiyyah's characterization of it as *ta'wīl* is notably precise.[98]

The Three Related Concepts: Essential Distinctions for Contemporary Application

Ibn Taymiyyah considered *tanqīḥ al-manāṭ, takhrīj al-manāṭ,* and *taḥqīq al-manāṭ* as "the essence of ijtihād."[99] Understanding their distinctions is crucial.

---

[92] Ibn Taymiyyah, *Majmū' al-Fatāwā, 19/16.*
[93] Al-Shāṭibī, *Al-Muwāfaqāt*, 4/90.
[94] Ibn Taymiyyah, *Majmū' al-Fatāwa*, 22/329.
[95] Ibn Taymiyyah, *Majmū' al-Fatāwa*, 22/330.
[96] Adapted, with minor stylistic changes, from 'Abd al-Qādir al-Tījānī's discussion of interpretive exegesis and political theory. 'Abd al-Qādir al-Tījānī, "Al-Tafsīr al-Ta'wīlī wa 'Ilm al-Siyāsah," *Al-Fikr al-Islāmī al-Mu'āṣir* 3, no. 10 (1997): 82-83.
[97] Ibn Taymiyyah, *Al-Radd 'alā al-Manṭiqiyyīn*, ed. Muḥammad Ḥasan Ismā'īl, 1st ed. (Beirut: Dār al-Kutub al-'Ilmiyyah, 1428 / 2007), 46.
[98] Farīd Shukrī, *Fiqh al-Tanzīl*, 1st ed. (Rabat: Maṭba'at al-Najāḥ al-Jadīdah, 2015), 47.
[99] Ibn Taymiyyah, *Majmū' al-Fatāwā*, 22/329. Understanding their distinctions proves essential for contemporary applications, as these three concepts form the methodological foundation for applying classical principles to novel circumstances.

Tanqīḥ al-Manāṭ (Refining the Effective Cause)

"When the Messenger ﷺ issues a ruling on a specific case, and we know that the ruling is not exclusive to that single case, then one aims to refine (*tanqīḥ*) the *manāṭ* of the ruling, to determine the type of case to which that ruling applies." This entails "pruning" the original *manāṭ*—separating it from descriptors that play no role in establishing the *'illa*.[100] Elsewhere he writes: "It is that he specified a ḥukm for specific entities, but we know that the ḥukm is not specific to them."[101]

Examples:

1. The Bedouin who had intercourse with his wife during Ramaḍān and was commanded to free a slave, fast two consecutive months, or feed sixty poor persons. The ḥukm is not confined to that individual; the question is whether the decisive factor was breaking the fast, intercourse in Ramaḍān, breaking the fast by intercourse, or a higher-order category.

2. The person entering *iḥrām* for ʿumrah wearing a shirt and perfumed with *khalūq*. The Prophet ﷺ said: "Remove your shirt, wash off the traces of perfume, and do in your ʿumrah what you would do in your ḥajj."[102] Is the washing mandated because *khalūq* is perfume (hence, any perfume must be removed by the *muḥrim*), or because *khalūq* is saffron-based and thus forbidden for men whether *muḥrim* or not?[103]

In sum, *tanqīḥ al-manāṭ* trims the original *manāṭ* until it is distinguished from attributes irrelevant to causation.

---

[100] Ibn Taymiyyah defines the concept in its derived form, insisting that the jurist must "yanqaḥ manāṭ al-ḥukm" ("refine the locus of the ruling"); this phrasing reflects his view that the criteria of inclusion and exclusion (al-jamʿ wa-l-manʿ) should not be shackled to Aristotelian logic. See Ibn Taymiyyah, *Majmūʿ al-Fatāwa*, 19/15.

[101] Ṣāliḥ Āl Manṣūr rejects this definition, arguing: "In my view the definition is flawed. It states that the Lawgiver explicitly assigns a ruling to specific cases… Once the Sharīʿah text specifies particular individuals, that very specification necessitates limiting the ruling to them. How, then, can one claim that the ruling is not confined to them? … It would be preferable to say that the ruling lies in the Lawgiver's assignment of the ruling to certain individuals, or that the Lawgiver links the ruling to its cause, so that attributes unrelated to that link must be set aside to widen the ruling." Ibn Taymiyyah, *Majmūʿ al-Fatāwā*, 22/230; Ṣāliḥ b. ʿAbd Allāh Āl Manṣūr, *Uṣūl al-Fiqh wa-Ibn Taymiyyah*, 2 vols. (Riyāḍ: Maktabat al-Rushd, 1424 / 2003), 1/382.

[102] The Prophet ﷺ instructed: "Remove your cloak, wash off the saffron dye, and whatever you intended to do for your ḥajj, do it instead in your ʿumrah." See: Ṣaḥīḥ Muslim, no. 1181.

[103] Ibn Taymiyyah, *Majmūʿ al-Fatāwa*, 22/328.

Takhrīj al-Manāṭ (Deriving the Effective Cause):

Ibn Taymiyyah writes: "As for *takhrīj al-manāṭ*, it is pure *qiyās*, and it is that he specifies a ḥukm for matters where one might think the ḥukm is specific to them, so one argues that others are like them, either due to the absence of a distinguishing factor, or due to sharing in the attribute for which evidence has been established that the lawgiver connected the ḥukm to in the original case."[104]

Here, the Sharīʿah has not explicitly stated the *ʿilla*, so the *mujtahid* infers it from the locus of the ḥukm, adopting the most fitting attribute in light of examination and division.

Examples:

1. Ribā was forbidden in wheat because it is a measured staple or an edible staple; thus rice is analogized to it.
2. The obligation of *ʿushr* (tithe) on wheat due to its status as a staple food—extending to other staples—or due to being a plant of the earth—extending to vegetables and similar produce.[105]

Taḥqīq al-Manāṭ (Verifying the Effective Cause)

In both *tanqīḥ* and *takhrīj*, engagement with the *manāṭ* occurs at the level of understanding the text. By contrast, *taḥqīq al-manāṭ* belongs to application (*tanzīl*): the *ʿilla* is known (by text or deduction), but one must ascertain its realization in the case at hand.

Certainty, Probability, and Contemporary Applications

Evidence for the occurrence of legal causes (*asbāb al-aḥkām*)—that is, *taḥqīq al-manāṭ*—ranges along a spectrum:

Evidence yielding certainty.

Causes whose occurrence and triggers are definitively known, e.g., onset of *Fajr* (the *manāṭ* for the obligation of *Ṣalāt al-Fajr*) or the passing of the sun's zenith (*zawāl*) for *Ẓuhr*. This is definitive, grounded in sense perception, observation, and experience.

---

[104] Ibn Taymiyyah, *Majmūʿ al-Fatāwa*, 19/17.

[105] Muḥammad b. Aḥmad al-Tinbuktī, *Al-Qawāʿid al-Uṣūlīyyah ʿinda Ibn Taymiyyah*, 2 vols. (Beirut: Dār Ibn Ḥazm, 1429 / 2008), 1:373.

Evidence yielding probability.

Causes whose existence is presumed based on indicators of varying strength, such as personal admission (*iqrār*), the testimony of four trustworthy witnesses, or oaths in litigation. These yield probability, not certainty.[106]

This distinction explains why refraining from applying a definitive text (*naṣṣ qaṭʿī*) to an incident that lacks the necessary conditions is *not* "ijtihād in the face of a definitive text," but ijtihād about the *ẓannī* dimension—namely, evidence for the incident's occurrence.[107]

This also clarifies certain ijtihādāt of ʿUmar ibn al-Khaṭṭāb (raḍiyallāhu ʿanhu), sometimes misread as opposing definitive texts, thereby giving pretext to suspend the Sharīʿah's *aḥkām*. Among these is his non-application of the *ḥadd* for theft during the year of famine.

This was not audacity toward the law but correct application (*tanzīl*): the *manāṭ* of theft was tainted by impurities that rendered it probabilistic. "He saw that the ḥukm did not apply to that situation, or that doubt affected the probability derived from the judicial procedures of proof in the case, so he repelled it. Thus, he applied a recognized doubt in neglecting a probability derived from the judicial process, and did not neglect the definitive text. His action was applying doubt in neglecting probability, not in rejecting certainty."[108]

ʿUmar (raḍiyallāhu ʿanhu) did not suspend a *ḥadd* whose conditions were fulfilled. Rather, holding—like many jurists—that *ḥudūd* are dropped by *shubuhāt*, he recognized the general famine as a pervasive doubt sufficient to suspend the penalty, as the thief in such circumstances most likely steals out of necessity.[109]

What ʿUmar (may Allah be pleased with him) did was not ijtihād against the text, that is, in opposition to the text, but rather ijtihād in understanding the text, which cannot be understood alone in isolation from the rest of the texts.

---

[106] Najm al-Dīn Qādir Karīm al-Zankī, *Qawāʿid al-Aḥkām*, 2 vols. (n.p.: n.d.), 2:33; *Al-Ijtihād fī Mawridi al-Naṣṣ: Dirāsah Uṣūlīyyah Muqāranah* (Beirut: Dār al-Kutub al-ʿIlmiyyah, 2006), 188.

[107] Al-Zankī, *Al-Ijtihād fī Mawridi al-Naṣṣ*, 189.

[108] Ibid.

[109] Yūsuf al-Qaraḍāwī, *Dirāsah fī Fiqh Maqāṣid al-Sharīʿah: Bayna al-Maqāṣid al-Kulliyyah wa-al-Nuṣūṣ al-Juzʾiyyah* (Cairo: Dār al-Shurūq, 2006), 107.

The texts collectively form the complete jurisprudential system related to implementing the ḥadd for theft, and through understanding them, the correct application of the ḥadd for theft is achieved. The ḥadd for theft has conditions that must be fulfilled and impediments that must be absent.[110]

Professor ʿAbd al-Majīd al-Najjār took a maqāṣidī (purposive) analysis of ʿUmar's ijtihād (may Allah be pleased with him), saying: "He knew the maqṣad (purpose) of the ḥukm and knew that it would not be realized in reality if the ḥukm of the ḥadd for theft were applied under famine conditions, so his knowledge of this was indicative of postponing the application."[111]

However, disagreement occurred regarding the position of the Commander of the Faithful ʿUmar (may Allah be pleased with him). In analyzing this, Shaykh al-Madanī says: "ʿUmar (may Allah be pleased with him) did not suspend a text here, nor did he modify or abrogate—far be it from him to see such a right for himself—but rather he understood that the taker of property in the year of famine cannot be described as a thief, because he sees for himself a right in what he takes, and theft is a person taking what he has no right to secretly."[112]

The Fundamental Importance for Contemporary Ijtihād

Ijtihād in *taḥqīq al-manāṭ* is central to Ibn Taymiyyah's *fiqh* and *uṣūl*. Acknowledging that "the lawgiver's texts are comprehensive words, universal propositions, and general rules, and it is impossible to specify every individual among the particulars of the world until the Day of Judgment,"[113] he affirms the inescapability of case-specific *ijtihād*: "So *ijtihād* regarding specific instances is necessary: do they fall under his comprehensive words or not?"[114]

Such *ijtihād* ensures the continuity and applicability of the Sharīʿah: "The *sharāʾiʿ* came with universal *aḥkām* such as obligating *zakāt* and prohibiting daughters and sisters. It is not possible to command anyone with what Allah commanded him and forbid him from what Allah forbade him unless one knows his inclusion in those universal categories... only with specific

---

[110] Muḥammad b. Aḥmad al-Tinbuktī, *Al-Qawāʿid al-Uṣūlīyyah ʿinda Ibn Taymiyyah* [Methodological Principles in Ibn Taymiyyah's Thought], 2 vols. (Beirut: Dār Ibn Ḥazm, 2008), 1:373.

[111] ʿAbd al-Majīd al-Najjār, *Maqāṣid al-Sharīʿah bi-Abʿād Jadīdah*, 2nd ed. (Beirut: Dār al-Gharb al-Islāmī, 2008), 20.

[112] Ibid, 108.

[113] Ibn Taymiyyah, *Minhāj al-Sunnah*, 6/139.

[114] Ibn Taymiyyah, *Minhāj al-Sunnah*, 6/139.

knowledge that this commanded thing falls under what Allah commanded, and this prohibited thing falls under what Allah forbade."[115]

"The specific particulars... such as the inheritance of this deceased person and the justice of this witness... and similar things, this is what no prophet, leader, or anyone among creation can specify regarding every individual case, because the actions and entities of human beings—their specific particulars exceed the knowledge and expression of any single human being. It is not possible for a human to know all of this through Allah's address to him. Rather, the possible maximum is mentioning universal, general matters."[116]

"The Book and Sunna clarified all the aḥkām through general names, but including specific entities in that requires precise understanding and penetrating insight, to include every specific entity under a category, and to include that category under another category that the Messenger ﷺ clarified. Then each of the incidents is encompassed by the Lawgiver's address and covered by sound consideration, and the Lawgiver's general, comprehensive address indicates them through the path of generality that refers back to taḥqīq al-manāṭ."[117]

The Importance of Knowing Taḥqīq al-Manāṭ for the Mujtahid:
Imām Ibn Taymiyyah gave taḥqīq al-manāṭ a normative function that enabled him to distinguish between fuqahāʾ. Therefore, he said: "As for knowing the inclusion of existing entities in these names and expressions, this may be apparent, and it may be hidden requiring ijtihād. This is the taʾwīl in the lawgiver's expression in which fuqahāʾ and others differ, for they have shared in memorizing the legal expressions with their names, or memorizing the speech of fuqahāʾ, grammarians, physicians, and others.

Then they differ in that one of them precedes in knowing that this existing specific entity is what is intended, or intended by this name. Just as the faqīh precedes regarding an incident and applies to it the lawgiver's speech or the jurist's speech... since books and speech transmitted from prophets and

---

[115] Ibn Taymiyyah, *Darʾ Taʿāruḍ al-ʿAql wa-al-Naql*, 6/387.
[116] Ibn Taymiyyah, *Minhāj al-Sunnah*, 6/413.
[117] Ibn Taymiyyah, *Darʾ Taʿāruḍ al-ʿAql wa-al-Naql*, 4/502.

scholars are absolute, mentioning things by their attributes and signs, so it is necessary to know that this specific entity is that one."[118]

Likewise: "The excellence of the *faqīh* when an incident occurs is that he perceives the inclusion of this incident under the general ḥukm that he and others know, or that they can know through its general evidence by text and deduction."[119]

Therefore, the fundamental nature of taḥqīq al-manāṭ in the ijtihād process is not hidden, because "knowing the legal evidence and its rank is part of what the mujtahid knows. It is not sufficient for being a mujtahid to know the genus of evidence; rather, he must know the specific instances of evidence. Whoever knows their specific instances and distinguishes between the specific instances of evidence and other things has better knowledge of their genus."[120]

It was mentioned previously that verificational ijtihād is necessary in all of sharīʿah because "the maximum the lawgiver can do is clarify the aḥkām through general, universal names, so knowledge of the inclusion of what is more specific than them—the categories and specific entities—under them"[121] only occurs through ijtihād in taḥqīq al-manāṭ, "for it is not possible to establish the ḥukm of a category or specific entity except through it."[122]

Based on Ibn Taymiyyah's discussion of taḥqīq al-manāṭ, the types of taḥqīq al-manāṭ can be limited to two types:

- Taḥqīq al-manāṭ in the scope of the **category** (*nawʿ*)
- Taḥqīq al-manāṭ in the scope of the **specific entity** (*ʿayn*)

Taḥqīq al-Manāṭ in the Scope of the Category

This form concerns universals and is applicable to multiple individuals. It is primary, since *taklīfī* rulings are abstract and general—unbounded by specific times, places, or persons, and encompassing both what is ruled upon and who

[118] Ibn Taymiyyah, *Al-Radd ʿalā al-Manṭiqiyyīn*, 46.
[119] Ibn Taymiyyah, *Bayān al-Dalīl*, 196.
[120] Ibn Taymiyyah, *Majmūʿ al-Fatāwa*, 20/402.
[121] Ibn Taymiyyah, *Darʾ Taʿāruḍ al-ʿAql wa-al-Naql*, 4/498.
[122] Ibid.

is ruled upon. Ibn Taymiyyah does not define it separately, but discusses it generally.[123]

Examples:

1. Determining whether liquids mixed with blood, carrion, or pork—where color and taste do not change and the impurities are absorbed or transformed—fall under the Qur'ānic/Sunnah designation of "water," or under "carrion," "blood," or "pork."[124]

2. Including intoxicants not derived from grapes/dates under *khamr*; including chess and backgammon under *maysir*; including racing without a mediator (*muḥallil*) in the rulings of horse-racing and archery; including sand among *ṣa'īd* in "Then perform *tayammum* with clean earth" (4:43); including one from whom corrupt semen has emerged in "But if you are in a state of *janāba*, then purify yourselves" (5:6); including the forearm in "Then wipe over your faces and your hands with it" (5:6); including the whiteness between the sideburn and ear within "Then wipe over your faces"; including water changed by pure things, or water touched by impurity that did not alter it, in "And you do not find water" (5:6); including the grave-robber within "As for the thief, the male and the female..." (5:38); including compulsory oaths within the designation of oaths; and including daughters' daughters and grandmothers within "Prohibited to you are your mothers..." (4:23).[125]

Taḥqīq al-Manāṭ in the Scope of the Specific Entity:

Categories verified by the law encompass countless individual actions. Though subsumed under a common category, each action is individuated and thus distinct, requiring *ijtihād* even more exacting than at the category level.[126]

This type of verificational ijtihād is the most frequent in Ibn Taymiyyah's discourse. He says: "As for the specific particulars—the particular whose conception prevents sharing in it, such as the inheritance of this deceased person, the justice of this witness, the maintenance of this wife, the occurrence

---

[123] Bashīr b. Maulūd Juḥaysh, *Fī al-Ijtihād al-Tanzīlī, Kitāb al-Ummah*, no. 93 (Doha: Wizārat al-Awqāf wa-al-Shu'ūn al-Islāmiyyah, 2003), 52.

[124] Ibn Taymiyyah, *Minhāj al-Sunnah*, 2/475.

[125] Ibn Taymiyyah, *Al-Radd 'alā al-Manṭiqiyyīn*, 47.

[126] *Adapted, with slight modification, from 'Abd al-Majīd al-Najjār's treatment of reason and revelation.* 'Abd al-Majīd al-Najjār, *Khilāfat al-Insān bayna al-Waḥy wa-al-'Aql* (Beirut: Dār al-Gharb al-Islāmī, 1987), 124.

of divorce by this husband, and implementing the ḥadd on this corruptor—this is what no prophet, leader, or anyone among creation can specify regarding every individual case, because the actions and entities of human beings—their specific particulars exceed the knowledge and expression of any single human being."[127] The specific prohibited things have no way to be specified by text, neither for a messenger nor a leader, but rather ijtihād is necessary in them.[128]

He defines it as such: "It is that the lawgiver has connected the ḥukm to an attribute, so we know its establishment regarding the specific individual."[129]

Examples:

— Determining the *qibla* amidst confusion;
— Establishing a person's justice;
— Assessing customary maintenance for a specific wife;
— Determining equivalents for game or destroyed property;
— Obligatory maintenance of kin;
— Including particular intoxicants within *khamr*;
— Including specific transactions within *ribā* or *maysir*.[130]

"It is like His command to seek witnesses of justice—when we know that this person is just, when we know that this specific individual is described with the justice mentioned in the Qur'ān."[131]

Special Taḥqīq al-Manāṭ in the Scope of the Specific Entity:

This verification is performed by the *mukallaf* himself, as he knows his own particularities best. He verifies the *manāṭ* of preference, since "the preferable varies according to the varying conditions of people... Among people are those for whom recitation is more beneficial than prayer, among them are those for whom *dhikr* is more beneficial than recitation, and among them are those for whom striving for the perfection of his necessity is better for him than *dhikr* in which he is heedless."[132]

[127] Ibn Taymiyyah, *Minhāj al-Sunnah*, 6/413.
[128] Ibn Taymiyyah, *Minhāj al-Sunnah*, 4/416.
[129] Ibn Taymiyyah, *Majmūʿ al-Fatāwa*, 13/254.
[130] Ibn Taymiyyah, *Darʾ Taʿāruḍ al-ʿAql wa-al-Naql*, 4/498.
[131] Ibn Taymiyyah, *Majmūʿ al-Fatāwa*, 13/254.
[132] Ibn Taymiyyah, *Majmūʿ al-Fatāwa*, 22/308.

Conclusion

Ultimately, the verification of effective legal causes (taḥqīq al-manāṭ) enables superior muwāzanāt by ensuring that balancing calculations operate upon accurate rather than presumptive foundations. When scholars engage in weighing competing interests without proper manāṭ verification, they risk applying classical rulings to contemporary situations that may appear similar but operate under fundamentally different causal dynamics.

For instance, the classical prohibition of ribā applies to specific economic relationships characterized by particular causal features (exploitation, wealth concentration, economic instability). Contemporary financial instruments may superficially resemble classical ribā scenarios while operating within different economic systems that alter the effective causes and consequences. Proper taḥqīq al-manāṭ requires scholars to verify whether the underlying causal mechanisms that originally justified specific rulings remain operative in contemporary contexts, or whether changed circumstances have altered the causal dynamics sufficiently to require modified legal analysis.

This verification process directly enhances muwāzanāt effectiveness by preventing the balancing of interests based on inaccurate assumptions about causal relationships, ensuring that benefit-harm calculations reflect actual rather than presumed consequences, and enabling more precise application of legal principles to contemporary scenarios. Without this verification step, even sophisticated balancing methodologies may produce flawed conclusions by operating on inapplicable causal assumptions.

Enhancing Muwāzanāt Effectiveness

Ibn Taymiyyah identified two primary types of *taḥqīq al-manāṭ*: category-level (*naw'*) verification determining whether contemporary phenomena fall under classical categories (e.g., modern intoxicants under *khamr*, contemporary gambling under *maysir*), and entity-specific (*'ayn*) verification involving individual determinations like witness credibility or customary maintenance amounts.[133] This verification process enables superior *muwāzanāt* by ensuring balancing calculations operate upon accurate rather than presumptive foundations, preventing misapplication of classical rulings

[133] Ibn Taymiyyah, *Dar' Ta'āruḍ al-'Aql wa-al-Naql*, 4:498; *Minhāj al-Sunnah*, 2:475. Category examples include "the inclusion of intoxicating drinks from other than grapes and dates under the designation of 'wine' (*khamr*), the inclusion of 'chess' and 'backgammon' and their like under the designation of 'gambling' (*maysir*)."

to situations that appear similar but operate under fundamentally different causal dynamics.[134]

Classical strategic alliances (*ḥilf*) with non-Muslims involved military cooperation, shared enemies, and mutual defense obligations potentially compromising religious principles, while contemporary multi-faith political coalitions operate through legislative advocacy, constitutional processes, shared policy objectives around social justice, and temporary cooperation preserving distinct religious identities, a distinction particularly evident in post-October 2023 dynamics revealing how pro-Israel lobbying organizations operate through institutional capture rather than traditional alliance structures.[135]

This verification process directly enhances *muwāzanāt* effectiveness by preventing interest-balancing based on inaccurate assumptions, ensuring benefit-harm calculations reflect actual dynamics of pluralistic advocacy rather than presumed parallels with classical alliances, and enabling precise application of cooperation principles to democratic coalition work where Muslims advance shared values while maintaining religious integrity.[136]

The necessity of *taḥqīq al-manāṭ* becomes particularly evident when examining artificial intelligence through an Islamic legal lens. Classical jurisprudence developed sophisticated frameworks for automation in various forms, like water mills for grain processing, mechanical devices for timekeeping, and irrigation systems operating without direct human intervention.

However, contemporary AI represents a qualitatively different phenomenon requiring careful verification of whether classical rulings on automation apply

---

[134] Without proper *manāṭ* verification, scholars risk applying classical rulings to contemporary situations based on superficial similarities while missing fundamental differences in underlying causal mechanisms.

[135] Specific examples include "*ijtihād* in determining the *qibla* when confused, *ijtihād* regarding the justice of a specific person, maintenance according to custom for a specific woman... the inclusion of types of intoxicants under the name of wine, and types of transactions under the name of *ribā* and gambling." Ibn Taymiyyah, *Majmūʿ al-Fatāwā*, 32:231; 22:308. For analysis of contemporary political dynamics, see Stephen Walt and John J. Mearsheimer, "The Israel Lobby and U.S. Foreign Policy," KSG Faculty Research Working Paper Series RWP06-011, March 2006.

[136] This contemporary application demonstrates how verification of effective legal causes ensures that Muslim organizations can navigate complex coalition politics with accurate understanding of partner constraints and genuine independence, rather than operating on assumptions derived from classical precedents involving fundamentally different power dynamics and alliance structures.

to systems exhibiting apparent decision-making capabilities.[137] The *manāṭ* (effective cause) of prohibitions against certain forms of delegation, for instance, centered on human agency and accountability. When AI systems make consequential decisions—loan approvals, medical diagnoses, or judicial recommendations—the question becomes whether the effective cause of human responsibility remains present when developers, users, and subjects of AI decisions are separated by layers of algorithmic complexity.[138]

This verification process proves equally crucial for digital matchmaking platforms. The classical prohibition of *khalwah* (inappropriate seclusion) between non-mahram individuals was predicated on preventing circumstances conducive to moral compromise. Digital communication presents scenarios that superficially resemble *khalwah*, such as private messaging, video calls, and intimate conversations, yet operate through fundamentally different causal mechanisms.[139]

The effective cause of the *khalwah* prohibition included physical proximity, absence of accountability, and environmental factors facilitating transgression. Digital interactions, while creating new forms of privacy, sometimes maintain records, enable monitoring (in some settings), and lack physical presence, but are oftentimes gateways to physical *khalwah* and gradual steps towards prohibited actions. Proper *taḥqīq al-manāṭ* requires examining whether these technological mediations alter the fundamental causal relationships that classical rulings addressed, neither hastily applying traditional categories to novel phenomena nor dismissing established principles without thorough investigation.

3.3. Condition III: Considering the Reality (Fiqh al-Wāqiʿ)

The Fundamental Importance of Contextual Understanding

A critical element in applying fiqh al-muwāzanāt is recognizing the role of context and reality in shaping the evaluation of interests. Ibn Taymiyyah emphasized this principle: "Whoever does not understand the reality (*al-*

[137] For contemporary AI and accountability, see Rahwan, Iyad. "Society-in-the-Loop: Programming the Algorithmic Social Contract." *Ethics and Information Technology* 20, no. 1 (2018): 5-14.

[138] On the complexities of algorithmic accountability in Islamic ethics, see Koca, Ozgur. "Artificial Intelligence and Islamic Ethics: Selected Preliminary Observations." *Journal of Islamic Ethics* 5, no. 1-2 (2021): 1-30.

[139] For classical discussions of khalwah, see al-Nawawī, Yaḥyā ibn Sharaf. *Rawḍat al-Ṭālibīn wa-ʿUmdat al-Muftīn*. Edited by Zuhayr al-Shāwīsh. Beirut: al-Maktab al-Islāmī, 1991, 7:19-23.

wāqiʿ) of creation and the obligation (*al-wājib*) in religion will not understand God's rulings concerning His servants. If one does not know these, then his words and deeds will be based on ignorance. And whoever worships God without knowledge does more harm than good."[140]

In this context, *wāqiʿ* refers to how a thing actually exists in its own context, irrespective of how it might be perceived or expressed by others.[141] This understanding requires deep engagement with empirical realities rather than theoretical abstractions. Another definition is that it is the fiqh of "descending to the field and observing the reality that people are in, and knowing their problems and their sufferings and their circumstances and what presents itself to them, and what are the texts that apply to their reality, in a particular stage, and what is deferred from the obligations to provide capability, this is indeed the jurisprudence of reality (fiqh al-wāqiʿ)."[142]

The Scholarly Imperative for Contextual Mastery

Among the established principles in Islamic scholarship is that passing judgment on a matter depends on proper understanding of it. Accurate legal rulings generally arise after thorough study of the issues presented to a muftī. A great *faqīh's* intimate familiarity with his society becomes clear to other scholars and students of knowledge who understand fiqh and its *uṣūl*, exemplified in every fatwā he issues. He speaks of people's affairs as if living continually among them, and he addresses their interests as though he were personally involved in their everyday interactions.

Some scholars were so committed to fiqh al-wāqiʿ that they made it a condition for being a jurist (*faqīh*). Al-Qarāfī said: "Applying rulings whose basis is customs when those customs have changed is contrary to consensus (*ijmāʿ*) and is ignorance in religion. Rather, everything in the Sharīʿah that follows customs: the ruling changes when the custom changes to what the new custom

---

[140] Ibn Taymiyyah, *Qāʿidah fī al-Maḥabbah*, In *Majmūʿ al-Fatāwā*, vol. 10. Medina: Majmaʿ al-Malik Fahd li-Ṭibāʿat al-Muṣḥaf al-Sharīf, 1995.

[141] It is mentioned in Lisān al-'Arab: "*waqa'a 'alā al-shay'* (it fell upon something), and from it *yaqa'u waqa'an wa-wuqū'an*: it fell, and likewise, *awqa'ahu ghayruh* (someone else made it fall), and *waqa'a al-maṭaru bi-al-arḍ* (the rain fell upon the earth)... and *mawāqi' al-ghayth* (places where rain falls): *masāqiṭuh* (its falling places), it is said *waqa'a al-shay' mawqi'ah* (the thing fell in its place)." See: *Kitāb al-'Ayn al-Muhmalah*, 8/402.

[142] *Fiqh al-Wāqi' Uṣūl wa-Ḍawābiṭ* (The Jurisprudence of Reality: Principles and Controls), Silsilat Kitāb al-Ummah, Issue No. 75 (Ministry of Awqāf and Islamic Affairs, Qatar, 2000), 44-45.

requires."[143] This emphasis reflects the recognition that legal reasoning disconnected from lived reality risks producing irrelevant or harmful guidance.

Contemporary AI deployment starkly illustrates why fiqh al-wāqiʿ remains indispensable for effective Islamic legal reasoning. The reality of AI implementation varies dramatically across contexts: facial recognition technology simultaneously serves legitimate security needs and enables authoritarian surveillance; large language models democratize access to information while amplifying misinformation; algorithmic content curation connects communities while creating echo chambers that polarize societies.[144]

Understanding these contextual variations requires scholars to engage deeply with technical specifications, deployment environments, and power structures governing AI systems. A ruling on AI-generated content, for instance, must account for differences between systems designed for creative expression versus those producing legal documents, medical advice, or religious guidance.[145]

Digital matchmaking platforms similarly demand sophisticated contextual analysis. The *wāqiʿ* of Muslim matrimonial searches encompasses diverse realities: converts lacking Muslim family networks, professionals whose careers limit traditional social circles, individuals with specific religious commitments seeking similarly-minded spouses, and those navigating cultural expectations while maintaining Islamic principles.[146] The proliferation of these platforms reflects broader social transformations, such as delayed marriage ages, geographic mobility, weakening extended family structures, and evolving gender roles in Muslim communities. Fiqh al-wāqiʿ requires recognizing that a platform's permissibility and optimal usage cannot be

---

[143] Shihāb al-Dīn Aḥmad b. Idrīs al-Qarāfī, *Al-Iḥkām fī Tamyīz al-Fatāwā ʿan al-Aḥkām wa-Taṣarrufāt al-Qāḍī wa-l-Imām*, ed. ʿAbd al-Fattāḥ Abū Ghuddah, 2nd ed. (Beirut: Dār al-Bashāʾir al-Islāmiyyah, 1995), 112.

[144] On AI's contextual variations and societal impact, see Crawford, Kate. *Atlas of AI: Power, Politics, and the Planetary Costs of Artificial Intelligence*. New Haven: Yale University Press, 2021. For echo chambers and polarization, see Sunstein, Cass R. *#Republic: Divided Democracy in the Age of Social Media*. Princeton: Princeton University Press, 2017.

[145] The need for contextual understanding in AI governance is emphasized in Jobin, Anna, Marcello Ienca, and Effy Vayena. "The Global Landscape of AI Ethics Guidelines." *Nature Machine Intelligence* 1, no. 9 (2019): 389-399.

[146] On convert experiences and marriage, see Roald, Anne Sofie. *New Muslims in the European Context: The Experience of Scandinavian Converts*. Leiden: Brill, 2004, especially chapter 6.

determined through abstract principles alone but demands understanding how these technologies function within specific social contexts, community norms, and individual circumstances.[147]

Ibn al-Qayyim said in the chapter on "The Change of Fatwās and Their Variation According to Changes in Times, Places, Conditions, Intentions, and Customs:"

> "This is a chapter of tremendous benefit. Ignorance of it has caused great error regarding the Sharīʿah, resulting in hardship, difficulty, and imposing what is impossible - things that one knows the brilliant Sharīʿah, which is at the highest levels of benefits, did not bring. The Sharīʿah is built and based on wisdom and the benefits of servants in this world and the next. It is all justice, all benefits, and all wisdom. Every issue that departs from justice to oppression, from mercy to its opposite, from benefit to harm, and from wisdom to futility is not from the Sharīʿah, even if it entered it through interpretation."[148]

The unprecedented consolidation of pro-Israel influence across American political institutions since October 2023, documented through congressional voting patterns showing near-unanimous support for military aid despite widespread public opposition, exemplifies how *fiqh al-wāqiʿ* must account for structural constraints that differ qualitatively from normal democratic pluralism. When both major political parties demonstrate systematic alignment with foreign state interests over domestic constituencies, traditional muwāzanāt calculations assuming meaningful electoral choice require fundamental recalibration.

3.4. Condition IV: Considering Consequences (Iʿtibār al-Maʾālāt) in Applying Rulings

The Domain of Practical Implementation

The consideration of consequences (iʿtibār al-maʾāl) fundamentally belongs to the domain of implementational reasoning (ijtihād tanzīlī). A key challenge for the legal scholar (mujtahid) lies not merely in examining present

[147] The transformation of Muslim marriage practices is analyzed in Mir-Hosseini, Ziba, and Richard Tapper. "Marriage, Family, and State: Changes in Shari'a-Based Family Law." In *The Oxford Handbook of Contemporary Islam*, edited by John L. Esposito and Emad El-Din Shahin. Oxford: Oxford University Press, 2014.

[148] Ibn al-Qayyim, *Iʿlām al-Muwaqqiʿīn ʿan Rabb al-ʿĀlamīn*, 3/3.

circumstances, but in anticipating probable outcomes—recognizing that a legal ruling might address an immediate benefit while potentially generating greater long-term harm.

Defining Consequential Reasoning

Iʿtibār al-maʾāl can be precisely defined as the comprehensive examination of an action's potential trajectories during the application of legal rulings. This encompasses both intended and unintended consequences, whether ultimately constructive or detrimental. [149] Dr. ʿAbd al-Raḥmān al-Sanūsī offers a particularly nuanced definition: "It is the verification of a ruling's foundational context (taḥqīq manāṭ al-ḥukm) by meticulously examining the consequential requirements that will emerge upon its application, assessing its capacity to achieve its fundamental objective (maqṣad), and systematically building upon those inherent necessities." [150]

Principles of Consequential Analysis

The principle of considering consequences represents a sophisticated form of applicational independent reasoning (ijtihād). [151] It necessitates that the legal scholar critically examine the potential outcomes of an action before rendering a definitive ruling. This approach prevents the mechanical application of textual injunctions to specific incidents, thereby avoiding unintended consequences that might contradict the lawgiver's fundamental intentions.

The foundational premise is elegantly straightforward: every legislative ruling is predicated on the benefits it generates in practical reality, just as prohibitions are established to prevent potential harms. The scholarly examination proceeds through a nuanced decision-making process:

1. When the potential benefits can be confidently anticipated, the action is deemed legitimate.
2. If the action fails to achieve its intended benefit or potentially generates greater harm, it may be prohibited.
3. Prohibitions are instituted to prevent harm, but only if the prevention does not create equivalent or escalated negative consequences. [152]

---

[149] ʿUmar Jadīyah, *Aṣl Iʿtibār al-Maʾāl bayna al-Naẓariyyah wa-al-Taṭbīq* (Beirut: Dār Ibn Ḥazm, 2009), 36.

[150] ʿAbd al-Raḥmān b. Maʿmar al-Sanūsī, *Iʿtibār al-Maʾālāt wa-Murāʿāt Natāʾij al-Taṣarrufāt: Dirāsah Muqāranah fī Uṣūl al-Fiqh wa-Maqāṣid al-Sharīʿah* (Dammām: Dār Ibn al-Jawzī, 1424 AH / 2003 CE), 19.

[151] Jadīyah, *Aṣl Iʿtibār al-Maʾāl bayna al-Naẓariyyah wa-al-Taṭbīq*, 55.

[152] Farīd Shukrī, *Fiqh al-Tanzīl*, 161.

A prime illustration of this methodology can be found in how the lawgiver "forbade prohibitions because they lead to corruption outside of them. Marrying two sisters is forbidden because it leads to severing kinship ties, and severing ties is a matter outside of marriage. Wine and gambling are forbidden and made abomination of Satan's work because that leads to turning away from prayer and causing enmity and hatred, which is a matter outside of wine and gambling. Ribā is forbidden because that leads to consuming wealth unjustly." [153]

Methodological Foundations

The methodology reflects a profound understanding of contextual complexity. As Ibn Taymiyyah eloquently articulates, the Sharīʿah fundamentally aims to:

- Achieve and perfect beneficial outcomes
- Nullify and minimize potential harms
- Prioritize the superior option between two positive alternatives
- Select the lesser harm when confronting conflicting negative potentialities[154]

He further notes a critical insight: "Many a principle, if its proponent knew what it leads to, he would not say it."[155] This approach demands that legal practitioners transcend immediate textual interpretations. A ruling's applicability is suspended until its comprehensive consequences are thoroughly verified. Even when an action satisfies all traditional causative conditions, potential negative implications might necessitate reconsideration.

Practical Implementation

The verification of consequences provides the legal scholar with a critical mechanism for: 1) Confirming the ruling's ultimate objective, 2) Ensuring the action genuinely serves its intended purpose, and 3) Tracing potential ripple effects across diverse contextual domains.[156]

Consider, for instance, the principle of forbidding wrongdoing: the intervention must be carefully calibrated to ensure it does not precipitate a

[153] Ibn Taymiyyah, *Majmūʿ al-Fatāwa*, 29/2287.
[154] Ibn Taymiyyah, *Majmūʿ al-Fatāwa*, 20/48.
[155] Ibn Taymiyyah, *Bayān al-Dalīl*, 147.
[156] Farīd Shukrī, *Fiqh al-Tanzīl*, 159-160.

more extensive or severe form of wrong.[157] Al-Shāṭibī's profound insight captures this methodological essence: "Considering the consequences of actions is an established and intended principle in the Sharī'ah, applicable whether actions align with or deviate from established norms. The scholar does not adjudicate any accountable person's action, whether proceeding or refraining, without meticulously and sincerely examining its potential consequences."[158]

Theological and Legal Rationale

The consideration of consequences is not merely a procedural technicality but reflects the Lawgiver's profound wisdom. As evidenced through rigorous inductive reasoning, the sharī'ah was established exclusively to serve human welfare in both temporal and spiritual dimensions. Allah's legislative framework systematically considers causative mechanisms and clarifies the intended purposes behind specific rulings.[159]

Ibn Taymiyyah illustrates this through contractual examples: "Allah legislated causes to be performed to achieve purposes, just as He legislated acts of worship from words and actions to seek His favor and pleasure, and just as He legislated the contract of sale to transfer ownership for compensation, the contract of loan to benefit the borrower, the contract of marriage for coupling and affection between spouses, *khul'* to achieve separation that includes the woman's ransom from her husband's authority, and other things," representing a dynamic, contextually sensitive methodology that transcends rigid literalism while emphasizing Islamic jurisprudence's adaptive and compassionate nature.[160]

[157] Ibn Taymiyyah, *Majmū' al-Fatāwa*, 22/191.
[158] al-Shāṭibī, *al-Muwāfaqāt*, 4/194-195.
[159] This theological foundation establishes that consequential analysis is intrinsic to divine legislation rather than a human addition to the interpretive process.
[160] Ibn Taymiyyah, *Bayān al-Dalīl*, 31. The enumeration of various contracts demonstrates how each legal institution serves specific purposive outcomes, reinforcing that Islamic law operates through goal-oriented rather than merely formal mechanisms.

Revelatory Evidence for Considering Consequences

The Qur'ān often justifies rulings by the outcomes to which they lead, making the consequence and recompense explicit:

1. Capital retribution: "There is life for you in *qiṣāṣ*, O people of discernment, so that you may be God-fearing."[161] Qiṣāṣ averts turmoil that would otherwise destroy society. Executing the murderer is in itself a harm (i.e., taking his life), yet it was permitted because it serves to preserve the lives of people at large.

2. Forbidding lawful acts when they lead to wrongdoing: "Do not revile those whom they invoke besides Allah, lest they revile Allah in enmity without knowledge"[162] Reviling idols is a form of worship, yet Allah forbade it because it would become a means to a worse evil, reviling Allah Himself.

3. Moderation in worship: "Do not raise your voice in prayer nor speak too softly, but seek a way between."[163] While in Mecca, the Prophet ﷺ was restrained from loud recitation lest the idolaters hear and blaspheme the Qur'ān, its Reveler, its recipient, and its bearer.

4. Likewise, the Prophet ﷺ consistently applied consequential reasoning, prohibiting what leads to prohibited outcomes ("A woman may not be married together with her paternal aunt or her maternal aunt") because such unions foster rivalry and eventual severing of kinship ties even if both women agree, and commanding "None of you should urinate in stagnant water and then wash in it" to "block the means," as urine causes impurity and successive urination further corrupts the water.[164]

The Foundations of Considering al-Ma'ālāt: Sadd al-Dharā'i'

Technical Definition: Dharī'ah as "whatever serves as a means or path leading to something."[165] The composite definition of *sadd al-dharā'i'* becomes: preventing whatever leads to a forbidden act. The purpose of *sadd al-dharā'i'* is to prevent avenues of corruption and block paths leading to it, preempting

---

[161] Qur'an 2:179.
[162] Qu'ran 6:108.
[163] Qur'an 17:110.
[164] Ṣaḥīḥ al-Bukhārī, no. 5109; Ṣaḥīḥ Muslim, no. 282. See Ibn Taymiyyah, *Bayān al-Dalīl*, 260; *Majmū' al-Fatāwa*, 21:34. These prophetic examples illustrate practical application of blocking means (*sadd al-dharā'i'*) to prevent harmful consequences, even when initial actions might appear permissible in isolation.
[165] Ibn Taymiyyah, *Bayān al-Dalīl*, 254.

it before it occurs. The Sharīʿah is built on caution and vigilance, preserving the aims (*maqāṣid*) of legislation. Therefore, *sadd al-dharāʾiʿ* is among the *uṣūl* (foundational principles) most closely connected to consequences (*maʾālāt*).

The relationship between *sadd al-dharāʾiʿ* and *maʾālāt* is causative. If a given means leads to evil, it is blocked, while if it leads to benefit or good, it is opened. The outcome (*maʾāl*) is the effect, and the *dharīʿah* is the cause. *Sadd al-dharāʾiʿ* is the most connected uṣūlī principle to consequences, and due to its strong connection to consequences, mention of consequences became associated with it.[166] To summarize, "when pure otherworldly benefits gather, if it is possible to achieve them all, we achieve them. If achieving them all becomes impossible, we achieve the most beneficial, then the more beneficial, then the most preferable, then the more preferable."[167]

The deployment of AI systems in critical domains exemplifies why considering consequences transcends theoretical exercise to become ethical imperative. When financial institutions implement AI-driven "halal lending" algorithms, immediate benefits include increased efficiency, reduced processing costs, and claims of objective decision-making. However, comprehensive analysis reveals cascading consequences: historical biases embedded in training data perpetuate discriminatory patterns, algorithmic opacity prevents applicants from understanding or contesting decisions, and the systematic exclusion of marginalized communities from capital access deepens economic inequalities.[168] The initial *maṣlaḥah* of efficiency transforms into compounded *mafsadah* when examining long-term societal impacts, particularly for communities already facing discrimination.[169]

Digital matchmaking platforms present equally complex considerations. While facilitating connections between compatible individuals across physical distances represents clear *maṣlaḥah*, the *maʾālāt* encompass broader societal

---

[166] Walīd b. ʿAlī al-Ḥusayn, *Iʿtibār Maʾālāt al-Afʿāl wa-Atharuhā al-Fiqhī*, 2 vols. (Riyāḍ: Dār al-Tadmuriyyah, 2009), 1:339.

[167] Ibn ʿAbd al-Salām, *Qawāʿid al-Aḥkām*.

[168] On algorithmic bias in lending, see Bartlett, Robert, et al. "Consumer-Lending Discrimination in the FinTech Era." *Journal of Financial Economics* 143, no. 1 (2022): 30-56. For the broader impact, see Barocas, Solon, and Andrew D. Selbst. "Big Data's Disparate Impact." *California Law Review* 104 (2016): 671-732.

[169] On Muslim experiences with financial discrimination, see Maurer, Bill. *Pious Property: Islamic Mortgages in the United States*. New York: Russell Sage Foundation, 2006.

transformations. The gamification of spouse selection through swipe-based interfaces cultivates consumerist attitudes toward marriage on some (but not all) platforms, where endless options paradoxically decrease satisfaction and commitment.[170] Platform algorithms optimizing for engagement metrics rather than marital success may promote superficial attractions over deeper compatibility. The normalization of presenting curated digital personas affects authenticity in initial interactions, potentially establishing relationships on foundations of mutual misrepresentation. Furthermore, the data collected through these platforms, like intimate preferences, private conversations, and behavioral patterns, creates vulnerabilities to exploitation, harassment, or surveillance that extend far beyond immediate matchmaking purposes.[171]

3.5. Condition V: The Jurisprudence of Priorities (Fiqh al-Awlawiyyāt)

Before engaging in *fiqh al-muwāzanāt*, contemporary Muslim scholars and legal councils must grasp the foundational discipline of *fiqh al-awlawiyyāt* (jurisprudence of priorities), which represents not merely academic nicety but essential methodological foundation without which legal balancing risks fundamental distortion of Islamic values and objectives.[172] The absence of this understanding has led to widespread confusion among contemporary religious movements, scholarly institutions, and Muslim communities, with well-intentioned practitioners expending enormous energy on secondary matters while neglecting fundamental obligations or elevating peripheral concerns above core principles.[173]

Many scholars identified a pervasive crisis of systematic priority inversion manifesting in troubling patterns: communities mobilizing extensive resources for mosque beautification while neglecting educational infrastructure;

---

[170] The paradox of choice in modern relationships is explored in Schwartz, Barry. *The Paradox of Choice: Why More Is Less*. New York: HarperCollins, 2004. On dating apps specifically, see Rosenfeld, Michael J., and Reuben J. Thomas. "Searching for a Mate: The Rise of the Internet as a Social Intermediary." *American Sociological Review* 77, no. 4 (2012): 523-547.

[171] On data vulnerabilities in dating platforms, see Lutz, Christoph, and Gemma Newlands. "Privacy and Smart Speakers: A Multi-Dimensional Approach." *The Information Society* 37, no. 3 (2021): 147-162. The specific risks for religious minorities are discussed in Noble, Safiya Umoja. *Algorithms of Oppression: How Search Engines Reinforce Racism*. New York: NYU Press, 2018.

[172] This prerequisite knowledge ensures that subsequent balancing exercises operate within properly understood value hierarchies rather than arbitrary preference systems.

[173] Contemporary inversions include Muslim organizations expending resources on interfaith dialogue events with groups actively supporting Palestinian erasure while neglecting urgent community needs like legal defense funds for students facing disciplinary actions for Palestine advocacy, illustrating misplaced priorities that favor symbolic acceptance over substantive justice.

scholarly debates consuming vast intellectual energy on peripheral ritual details while fundamental questions of necessities remain unaddressed; and movements prioritizing symbolic piety over substantive engagement with poverty, ignorance, and structural violence.[174] This misallocation stems from fundamental misunderstanding of Islamic obligations' hierarchical nature, as the Qur'ān establishes:

أَجَعَلْتُمْ سِقَايَةَ ٱلْحَآجِّ وَعِمَارَةَ ٱلْمَسْجِدِ ٱلْحَرَامِ كَمَنْ ءَامَنَ بِٱللَّهِ وَٱلْيَوْمِ ٱلْـَٔاخِرِ وَجَٰهَدَ فِى سَبِيلِ ٱللَّهِ ۚ لَا يَسْتَوُۥنَ عِندَ ٱللَّهِ ۗ وَٱللَّهُ لَا يَهْدِى ٱلْقَوْمَ ٱلظَّٰلِمِينَ

"Do you consider providing the pilgrims with water and maintaining the Sacred Mosque as equal to believing in Allah and the Last Day and struggling in the cause of Allah? They are not equal in Allah's sight."[175]

Theoretical Foundations: Quality over Quantity

The Islamic tradition consistently emphasizes qualitative over quantitative measures of religious achievement. The hadith that "actions are but by intentions"[176] establishes intention and purpose as the primary criterion for evaluating religious acts, superseding mere volume or frequency of practice. This principle extends beyond individual worship to encompass communal religious life. A small number of deeply committed believers working with clear priorities and strategic thinking contributes more to Islamic civilization than masses engaged in unfocused activity. The Qur'ānic praise for *"those who remember Allah standing, sitting, and lying on their sides and give thought to the creation of the heavens and earth"*[177] emphasizes reflective quality over mechanical repetition.

---

[174] Yūsuf al-Qaraḍāwī, *Fī Fiqh al-Awlawiyyāt.* These patterns reflect not individual failings but systematic educational and institutional deficiencies in teaching priority frameworks.

[175] Qur'an 9:19. This verse explicitly rejects equivalence between acts of different religious significance, establishing divine precedent for hierarchical evaluation of religious actions.

[176] Ṣaḥīḥ al-Bukhārī, no. 54, Ṣaḥīḥ Muslim, no. 1907.

[177] Qur'an 3:191.

Examples of Prioritization Principles

Although beyond this book's scope, the following principles exemplify the field requiring mastery for effective interest-balancing, similar to Condition I:

A. Theological and Creedal Priorities
   1. Fundamentals over Secondary Issues[178]
   2. Certainty over Probability[179]

B. Practical and Ritual Priorities
   3. Obligations over Voluntary Acts[180]
   4. Individual vs. Communal Obligations[181]

C. Social and Ethical Priorities
   5. Human Rights in Relation to Divine Rights[182]
   6. Community over Individual Interests[183]

D. Methodological and Epistemological Priorities
   7. Knowledge before Action[184]

---

[178] Islamic theology establishes an unambiguous hierarchy wherein matters of ʿaqīdah (creed) and īmān (faith) take absolute precedence over practical jurisprudential details. The Qur'ānic sequence consistently places belief before action: "Those who believe and do righteous deeds." This ordering reflects not mere literary convention but fundamental theological priority. Contemporary application requires that educational curricula, community programs, and scholarly research prioritize developing sound Islamic worldview and character formation before advancing to complex legal opinions on secondary matters.

[179] Definitive (*qaṭʿī*) textual evidence takes precedence over probable (*ẓannī*) interpretations. This principle prevents the elevation of disputed scholarly opinions to the level of fundamental religious requirements, maintaining essential flexibility in areas where the divine guidance allows for interpretive diversity.

[180] The foundational principle that required duties (farāʾiḍ) supersede recommended practices (sunan and nawāfil) appears throughout Islamic literature. The Prophet emphasized: "My servant does not draw near to Me with anything more loved by Me than the religious duties I have imposed upon him" (Bukhārī). This principle revolutionizes contemporary religious practice by redirecting energy from accumulating voluntary acts toward perfecting obligatory duties, both ritual and social.

[181] Personal obligatory duties (farḍ ʿayn) take precedence over collective responsibilities (farḍ kifāyah), though this hierarchy operates within careful parameters. An individual must fulfill personal obligations before contributing to communal needs, yet when communal obligations remain completely unmet, they may supersede individual voluntary acts.

[182] Islam establishes a nuanced relationship between divine rights (*ḥuqūq Allah*) and human rights (*ḥuqūq al-ʿibād*). While divine rights hold ultimate priority, the tradition demonstrates remarkable flexibility in cases where human welfare demands immediate attention. The Prophet's permission to break voluntary fasts when guests arrive exemplifies this principle. The general rule holds that human rights often take practical precedence because: (a) God is self-sufficient and does not benefit from worship, while humans suffer harm from neglect; (b) human rights typically cannot be forgiven except by their holders, while divine forgiveness is accessible; and (c) fulfilling human rights often constitutes worship of the highest order.

[183] The welfare of the Muslim community (*ummah*) supersedes individual interests when genuine conflict arises. This principle, rooted in the Qur'ānic vision of Muslims as a *"middle nation"* (*ummatan wasaṭan*), provides the foundation for legitimate governmental authority and social legislation. However, this principle requires careful application to prevent authoritarian abuse. Individual rights retain strong protection, and communal interests must represent genuine benefit rather than elite manipulation.

[184] The command *"So know that there is no deity except Allah, then seek forgiveness"* (47:19) establishes knowledge as the prerequisite for all righteous action. This principle applies to both religious and worldly affairs, demanding that individuals and communities invest in understanding before implementing.

8. Understanding over Memorization[185]

9. Purposive Interpretation over Literalism[186]

10. Independent Reasoning over Blind Following[187]

E. Temporal and Contextual Priorities

11. Permanent over Temporary Benefits[188]

12. Widespread over Limited Benefit[189]

13. Actions in Times of Crisis[190]

14. Heart over Limbs[191]

Implications for Contemporary Islamic Discourse

The systematic application of *fiqh al-awlawiyyāt* would revolutionize contemporary Islamic practice and scholarship: religious institutions prioritizing character development over ritual compliance monitoring, Islamic education emphasizing critical thinking over textual memorization, and Muslim communities focusing on fundamental social problems rather than symbolic religious displays.[192]

For legal councils and scholarly bodies, mastery of these priorities becomes essential before attempting complex balancing between competing interests, as without this foundation, *fiqh al-muwāzanāt* risks becoming mere

[185] While memorization of Islamic texts holds great value, comprehension and internalization take priority over mere textual retention. The Qur'ānic criticism of those who *"carry the Torah but do not act upon it, like a donkey carrying books"* (Al-Jumuʿah 62:5) warns against emphasizing form over substance.

[186] Understanding the objectives of Islamic legislation takes precedence over rigid adherence to apparent textual meanings when these conflict. This principle, developed systematically by scholars like al-Shāṭibī, prevents the manipulation of Islamic texts to achieve outcomes contrary to their underlying purposes.

[187] While respecting scholarly tradition, contemporary Muslim scholarly councils must prioritize independent reasoning (*ijtihād*) over blind following (*taqlīd*) when facing novel, challenging circumstances. The Prophet's declaration that *"scholars are the inheritors of the prophets"* implies the continuation of interpretive responsibility, not its termination.

[188] Actions whose benefits continue beyond their immediate timeframe take precedence over those with temporary impact. The concept of *ṣadaqah jāriyah* (continuing charity) exemplifies this principle, as does investment in education over immediate consumption.

[189] Actions benefiting broader populations supersede those with restricted impact. This principle elevates public service, education, and social reform above purely personal spiritual practices.

[190] Righteous action during periods of tribulation, oppression, or social decline carries enhanced merit and priority due to its increased difficulty and greater social necessity. The principle finds its apex in numerous reports, such as: "The best jihād is a truthful word before an unjust ruler" (Abū Dāwūd, al-Tirmidhī). The Prophet further declared: "The master of martyrs is Ḥamzah ibn ʿAbd al-Muṭṭalib, and a man who stood before an unjust imam, commanded him to good and forbade him from evil, and was killed for it." The Prophet also provided quantitative perspective on this principle: "Worship during tribulation (harj) is like emigration to me" (Muslim)

[191] Internal spiritual states and intentions (*ʿamal al-qalb*) take precedence over external ritual actions (*ʿamal al-jawāriḥ*), since the latter derive their validity from the former. The Prophet's emphasis on the heart as *"the piece of flesh that, if it is sound, the whole body is sound"* establishes this hierarchy.

[192] This transformation would redirect religious energy from performative demonstrations toward substantive engagement with community needs and societal challenges.

preference-based decision-making rather than principled Islamic jurisprudence.[193] The revival of authentic *fiqh al-awlawiyyāt* represents not academic luxury but existential necessity for contemporary Islamic civilization, as Muslim communities worldwide grappling with complex social, political, and economic challenges require the ability to distinguish between essential and peripheral concerns for effective religious, social, and political leadership.[194]

The rapid advancement of artificial intelligence demands sophisticated priority assessment distinguishing between critical interventions and peripheral concerns. While some Muslim discourse fixates on whether AI-generated art violates prohibitions against image-making, more fundamental questions demand urgent attention: the use of AI in autonomous weapons systems directly impacts *ḥifẓ al-nafs* (preservation of life), algorithmic bias in judicial systems affects the establishment of justice, and AI-driven surveillance technologies threaten the basic human dignity that Islamic law seeks to protect.[195] Fiqh al-awlawiyyāt requires prioritizing engagement with AI applications that affect *ḍarūriyyāt* over those merely impacting *taḥsīniyyāt*, directing scholarly attention and community resources toward the most consequential developments rather than marginal applications.[196]

The primary fiqhi claim of this book is that daily-use AI should be evaluated as a morally consequential technology whose ruling depends not only on the user's immediate intention, but also on the nature of the use case, the rights implicated, the harms facilitated, the system's design, the probability and severity of consequences, and the availability of safer alternatives. A daily-use AI application may be permissible when it assists a lawful purpose without deception, harm, dependency, privacy violation, or unlawful exposure. It may be disliked when it weakens discipline, replaces healthier human relationships,

---

[193] The prerequisite nature of priority understanding ensures that subsequent balancing exercises operate within divinely established value hierarchies rather than subjective preferences or cultural biases.

[194] Contemporary examples include determining whether resources should address immediate humanitarian crises or long-term educational infrastructure, whether political engagement should prioritize symbolic victories or substantive policy changes, and whether interfaith activities should focus on theological dialogue or collaborative justice work.

[195] On AI weapons and Islamic ethics, see Khan, M. A. Muqtedar. "Artificial Intelligence, Autonomous Weapons and Islamic Ethics." *Journal of Islamic and Muslim Studies* 4, no. 1 (2019): 84-102. For the broader framework of human dignity in Islamic law, see Sachedina, Abdulaziz. *Islam and the Challenge of Human Rights*. Oxford: Oxford University Press, 2009.

[196] The principle of prioritizing essential over peripheral concerns reflects the methodology outlined in al-Qaraḍāwī, Yūsuf. *Awlawiyyāt al-Ḥaraka al-Islāmiyya fī al-Marḥala al-Qādima*. Cairo: Maktabat Wahba, 1991.

or habituates morally corrosive patterns. It may be prohibited when it enables falsehood, impersonation, sexualized interaction, betrayal of trust, academic fraud, violation of privacy, or foreseeable harm to individuals or the public. Such gradation is not indecision. It is the ordinary work of iftā'' when a single technology contains multiple possible uses, contexts, and consequences.

Digital matchmaking platforms similarly require priority-based analysis distinguishing essential concerns from secondary considerations. While debates arise regarding profile photo permissibility or specific interface features, *awlawiyyāt* directs attention to more fundamental issues: protecting vulnerable users from exploitation, ensuring platforms facilitate marriages aligned with Islamic objectives rather than merely enabling encounters, and addressing how these technologies reshape community marriage practices and expectations.[197] The priority remains safeguarding and facilitating the institution of marriage as a means of achieving tranquility and establishing righteous families, rather than becoming preoccupied with peripheral platform features that minimally impact these core objectives.

While Dr. al-Qaraḍāwī's foundational work provides an essential starting point for this revival in our times, contemporary scholars must extend and apply these principles to emerging twenty-first century challenges, enabling the Islamic legal tradition to contribute meaningfully to contemporary debates through sophisticated *fiqh al-muwāzanāt* methodology, ultimately realizing Islam's comprehensive vision: societies embodying divine guidance through human institutions where individual spiritual development and communal welfare achieve harmonious integration under revealed priorities' clear hierarchy.[198]

---

[197] On protecting vulnerable users online, see Boyd, Danah. *It's Complicated: The Social Lives of Networked Teens*. New Haven: Yale University Press, 2014. While focused on teens, the vulnerability frameworks apply to other populations navigating digital spaces.

[198] This vision transcends both secular materialism and otherworldly escapism, offering a balanced approach that honors both spiritual and temporal dimensions of human existence within properly understood priority frameworks.

4

The Balancing Act: Al-Muwāzanah wal-Tarjīḥ (Balancing and Prioritizing)

"As for prioritizing the ranks of recognized good (ma'rūf) and evil (munkar) and the degrees of evidence (dalīl), so that, in case of conflict, you give precedence to the most pressing good and call to it, oppose the most severe evil and forbid it, and likewise give preference to the stronger of two evidences—that is the hallmark of those most learned in this religion." – Ibn Taymiyyah[199]

Al-muwāzanah (weighing and balancing considerations) is one of the most intricate and challenging tasks a jurist undertakes. It guides him when interests (*maṣāliḥ*) clash with one another, or harms (*mafāsid*) collide, or when interests and harms oppose each other. He must place everything in its proper rank justly, whether rulings, values, or actions, then prioritize them correctly based on proper Shar'ī standards, informed by both revelation and reason. Rather, he gives precedence to whatever truly merits precedence, and postpones what belongs later, avoiding magnifying what is minor or downplaying what is significant. Instead, everything is put in its rightful place with the perfect "balance" (*al-qisṭās al-mustaqīm*), free of either excess or neglect, as God says: "And He raised the heaven and established the balance, so that you may not transgress within the balance. And establish weight with justice and do not decrease the balance."[200]

---

[199] Ibn Taymiyyah, *Majmū' al-Fatāwā*, ed. 'Abd al-Raḥmān ibn Qāsim, 37 vols. (al-Manṣūrah: Dār al-Wafā', 2005).
[200] Qur'an 55:7-9.

This chapter presents the actual balancing act (*muwāzanah*), covering three types and their applications to Muslim American political engagement:

1. The balancing of benefits (muwāzanat al-maṣāliḥ)
2. The balancing of harms (muwāzanat al-mafāsid)
3. The balancing between benefits and harms (muwāzanat al-maṣāliḥ wa al-mafāsid)

Typologies of Fiqh al-Muwāzanāt

Before diving into the three typologies, it is crucial to emphasize what should be apparent to every sincere and wise believer. When engaging in muwāzanah (the balancing of maṣāliḥ and mafāsid), the first step is to actually verify that each interest presented is genuine. The scholar must, with honesty and objectivity, distinguish between legitimate maṣlaḥah and anything that is imagined, fabricated, or already nullified by sharīʿah. Any interest found to be illusory or contradicted by established rulings must be set aside and not weighed against real considerations.

Once authenticity is confirmed, the scholar should attempt to reconcile all valid interests rather than neglect one in favor of another. Combining maṣāliḥ is preferred whenever possible; for example, by comparing their temporal scope, availability of substitutes, and the legislator's implicit ordering, so long as they do not truly conflict. Muwāzanāt remains an exception to the general rule of fulfilling all obligations, employed only when interests cannot coexist.

4.1. The Balancing of Benefits (al-Maṣāliḥ)

When two interests (*maṣāliḥ*) conflict, the jurist gives precedence to the more important over the less important, the obligatory over the recommended, the essential (*ḍarūrī*) over the complementary (*ḥājī*) and the embellishing (*taḥsīnī*), prioritizing communal interests over individual ones, lasting interests over temporary ones, and the more certain interests over those that are merely probable.[201]

Revelatory Evidence

Revelatory evidence in Sūrat Ṭāhā demonstrates this principle when Hārūn (AS) explains to Mūsā (AS) why he did not more forcefully restrain the Banū Isrāʾīl from wrongdoing in Mūsā's absence, stating his forbearance was due to

[201] This hierarchical framework provides systematic criteria for resolving conflicts between competing beneficial outcomes, ensuring decisions align with Islamic value structures rather than arbitrary preferences.

preserving the community's unity until Mūsā's return, tolerating a lesser wrong temporarily to avoid the far graver consequence of outright schism among the Israelites, highlighting how prioritizing unity can sometimes necessitate postponing immediate corrective measures when such measures risk inciting more severe divisions.[202]

Likewise, the Prophet ﷺ established this principle through statements like "Ṣalāh in congregation is superior to ṣalāh performed alone by twenty-seven degrees" and "Guarding (*ribāṭ*) for a day or a night in the cause of Allāh is better than fasting for an entire month and performing its nightly prayers," demonstrating how fulfilling certain religious responsibilities, such as defending the community, can take precedence over other meritorious acts like voluntary fasting and night prayers, thus exemplifying balancing benefits in various forms of worship.[203]

Guidelines for Balancing Benefits

Scholars have offered guidelines (*ḍawābiṭ*) for balancing between interests, such as 'Izz al-Din's guidelines on seven maxims,[204] including some of the following:

1. Prioritizing by the Rank of the Ruling

The *wājib* (obligatory) would be preferred over the *mandūb* (recommended), as in prioritizing the repayment of a demanded debt over giving voluntary charity.[205] Similarly, a *farḍ 'ayn* (individual obligation) is preferred over a *farḍ kifāyah* (communal obligation). This also includes examples of ranking in terms of value or noble actions, such as obedience to Allah above obedience to creation, and prioritizing necessities before needs and embellishments.

2. Prioritizing by Scope (Individual vs. Collective)

The public interest is preferred over a private one, such as price regulation in times of inflation. If hoarding or similar practices cause deliberate price hikes,

---

[202] Qur'an 20:94. This Qur'ānic account provides divine precedent for sophisticated consequential reasoning where immediate action might produce greater harm than temporary forbearance.

[203] Ṣaḥīḥ al-Bukhārī, no. 649; no. 2892. These prophetic comparisons establish quantitative relationships between different acts of worship, providing practical guidance for prioritizing religious obligations based on their relative merit and communal impact.

[204] See 'Izz al-Dīn 'Abd al-Salām, *Qawā'id al-Aḥkām.* The seven maxims are not listed in order here but repurposed for the three classifications of interests, harms, and interests v. harms.

[205] Ibn Taymiyyah, *Majmū' al-Fatāwa*, 20/51.

the ruler imposes fixed pricing, even if it harms one seller, because his loss is an individual matter, whereas communal good is a collective interest.[206]

Another example Ibn Taymiyyah cites concerns an imam adjusting his practice in congregational prayer to avoid dissension. Suppose the imam believes it is superior (*afḍal*) to separate the witr (prayer) into two rakʿahs plus one (rejecting the view that sees it as a single continuous set), but the congregation strongly believes in a single continuous witr. In that case, the imam can opt for the second method to preserve unity.

This is *mushārakah* in a less preferred method for the sake of a stronger communal interest: harmony. The same reasoning applies if he believes it is more correct to recite the *basmalah* loudly, while the congregation holds otherwise, or vice versa.[207] Doing the less preferred act, therefore, can become preferred if it serves a great unifying benefit.[208] It is a given that these statements of Ibn Taymiyyah refer only to situations where there is flexibility and validity in the fiqh opinions in a given context.

For instance, the development of AI capabilities presents contemporary Muslims with complex benefit-balancing scenarios. Consider the choice between developing AI systems for Islamic education versus healthcare applications. Educational AI offers benefits including personalized Islamic learning, 24/7 availability for religious questions, and preservation of scholarly knowledge through digital encoding. Healthcare AI promises earlier disease detection, optimized treatment protocols, and expanded medical access to underserved Muslim communities.[209] Both serve legitimate *maṣāliḥ*, yet resource constraints often demand prioritization. The balancing calculation must weigh factors including scope of impact (healthcare affecting ḥifẓ al-nafs more directly), replaceability (human teachers remain available while medical specialists are scarce), and temporal urgency (immediate health needs versus long-term educational development).[210]

---

[206] Ibn Taymiyyah, *Majmūʿ al-Fatāwa*, 29/256.

[207] Ibn Taymiyyah, *Majmūʿ al-Fatāwa*, 24/195.

[208] Ibn Taymiyyah, *Majmūʿ al-Fatāwa*, 22/344.

[209] On AI in Islamic education, see Bunt, Gary R. *Hashtag Islam: How Cyber-Islamic Environments Are Transforming Religious Authority*. Chapel Hill: University of North Carolina Press, 2018. For healthcare applications, see Topol, Eric. *Deep Medicine: How Artificial Intelligence Can Make Healthcare Human Again*. New York: Basic Books, 2019.

[210] The framework for technology resource allocation in Muslim contexts needs development. For general principles, see Masud, Muhammad Khalid. "The Doctrine of Siyāsa in Islamic Law." *Recht van de Islam* 18 (2001): 1-29.

Digital matchmaking platforms force Muslim communities to balance between preserving traditional community-mediated introductions and embracing technological solutions. Traditional methods offer benefits of family knowledge, community accountability, and established vetting processes. Digital platforms provide expanded choice, geographic reach, and autonomy for individuals whose families may not share their religious priorities, as well as for expanding networks in societies where Muslims are minorities and options are limited. When communities must allocate resources and religious sanction between developing digital infrastructure versus strengthening traditional institutions, the muwāzanah requires evaluating which approach better serves the fundamental objective of facilitating righteous marriages in contemporary contexts where both methods offer distinct, partially overlapping benefits.[211]

3. Choosing What Benefits the Individual

If two personal advantages clash, choose the one that yields greater benefit to that individual. As Ibn Taymiyyah notes, a single person's condition varies, but the best deed is what is most obedient to Allah and brings the greatest benefit to its doer. That might be the simpler or the tougher of two actions; not every demanding task is better, nor every easy task inferior.[212]

An apparently "inferior" deed might actually be superior for a given individual if he benefits more from it. For example, if someone has already memorized enough Qur᾽ān for his needs but lacks certain other knowledge, then learning that additional needed science is better than repeating Qur᾽ān he does not require (to worship), or if he knows some Qur᾽ān but does not understand it, studying its meaning is better than merely reciting words he does not comprehend.[213]

Likewise, a person might be unable to perform the "best" action in its full manner, like someone who cannot fully memorize the Qur᾽ān or do a certain worship at its highest standard, yet might excel in a lesser act. Hence, not every act that is objectively superior is required of every individual. One must select

---

[211] The concept of maṣlaḥa in contemporary contexts is thoroughly examined in Opwis, Felicitas. *Maṣlaḥa and the Purpose of the Law: Islamic Discourse on Legal Change from the 4th/10th to 8th/14th Century*. Leiden: Brill, 2010.

[212] Ibn Taymiyyah, *Majmūʿ al-Fatāwa*, 22/313.

[213] Ibn Taymiyyah, *Majmūʿ al-Fatāwa*, 23/56.

the best act for oneself, given one's capacity. For some, charity might be better than extra fasting, or hajj might be better than jihad (e.g., women, or those physically unable to fight), even though jihad is generally more meritorious.[214] Importantly, we must not confuse excellence with difficulty. Nor do actions differ by quantity alone; they vary in how they impact the heart.[215]

4. Prioritizing by Potential Replacement

If you must choose between two benefits and performing one forfeits the other, and if one can be replaced but the other cannot, then prioritize the one whose loss cannot be remedied. This is summarized by the principle: "If one of two gains will be lost irrecoverably, and the other, though lost, can be compensated, then we secure that which has no substitute and let go of the one which can be replaced."[216]

Likewise, if two good deeds conflict, one of which must be done now or not at all, while the other can be performed later, one must engage in the act that cannot be postponed. For instance, one might respond to the *mu'adhdhin* during the *adhān*, or pray the solar eclipse prayer (*kusūf*) over other concurrent but deferrable acts.[217]

4.2. The Balancing of Harms (al-Mafāsid)

If two evils (*mafāsid*) conflict in a setting where both cannot be avoided, one must ward off the worse by tolerating the lesser, never repelling small evil by causing larger evil nor removing lighter harm by producing greater harm, thus whatever cannot be wholly removed of evil must be diminished as much as possible, with the lesser of two evils not being truly *ḥarām* in this case though described as prohibited in general contexts.[218]

Revelatory evidence in Sūrat al-Kahf shows al-Khaḍir damaging a boat to save it from confiscation by a king seizing all usable vessels, choosing lesser harm (partial damage) over greater harm (complete loss to tyranny).[219]

---

[214] Ibn Taymiyyah, *Majmū' al-Fatāwa*, 23/60.
[215] Ibn Taymiyyah, *Majmū' al-Fatāwa*, 25/281.
[216] Nāṣir al-Mīmān, *Al-Qawā'id wa-al-ḍawābiṭ al-fiqhiyya 'inda Shaykh al-Islām Ibn Taymiyya fī Kitābay "al-Ṭahārah wa-al-Ṣalāh"* (Master's thesis, Umm al-Qurā University, 1993), 1/479.
[217] Nāṣir al-Mīmān, *Al-Qawā'id,* 1/480. This refers to the maxim: إذا تزاحمت مصلحتان إحداهما تفوت والأخرى لا تفوت، قدمت التي تفوت على التي لا تفوت
[218] Ibn Taymiyyah, *Majmū' al-Fatāwa*, 23:343; 20:57. This principle establishes that context transforms the legal status of actions, where normally prohibited acts become permissible when preventing greater harm.
[219] Qur'an 18:79. This divine narrative provides Qur'ānic precedent for preemptive action causing minor harm to prevent major loss.

Likewise, the Prophet's ﷺ instruction regarding the Bedouin man urinating in the mosque, "Let him be, and do not interrupt him," exemplifies preventing greater harm through accepting lesser harm, as interruption might have caused physical harm, further soiling, or alienation from Islam, with Ibn Ḥajar noting: "The Prophet did not reprimand the companions for their initial reaction but instructed them to cease for the greater benefit, exemplifying the principle of choosing lesser harm to avoid greater harm and securing greater benefit by abandoning a lesser one."[220]

Another evidence for prioritizing the lesser harm includes the ḥadīth in which ʿUmar (rA) said: "The Prophet ﷺ once divided some spoils, and I (ʿUmar) remarked, 'O Messenger of God, others are more deserving than these people.' The Prophet ﷺ replied, *'They have forced me to choose between rude demands and being labeled a miser, and I refuse to be a miser.'*"[221]

Ibn Taymiyyah explains: "…they force me into one of two disliked outcomes, bad language on their part or me being called miserly. The latter is more severe, so I repel the more severe by giving (war spoils) to them."[222]

Another evidence from the companions is the statement from Ibn Masʿūd and Ibn ʿAbbās (rA): "I would rather swear by Allah while lying than swear by someone else truthfully." Swearing by other than Allah is shirk, and shirk is worse than lying. Thus, they prioritized preserving tawḥīd over preserving perfect truthfulness, because shirk is a far graver evil.[223]

Similarly, the Prophet ﷺ and his Companions were gladdened by the Romans' victories over the Persians, even though both sides were disbelievers, because the Romans were closer to Islam than the Zoroastrians.[224]

---

[220] Ṣaḥīḥ al-Bukhārī, no. 6025; Ibn Ḥajar, *Fatḥ al-Bari*, 1:324. The Prophet's wisdom in allowing temporary ritual impurity to prevent permanent spiritual alienation demonstrates practical application of harm minimization.

[221] Ṣaḥīḥ Muslim, no. 1056.

[222] Ibn Taymiyyah, *Majmūʿ al-Fatāwa*, 28/155.

[223] Nāṣir al-Mīmān, *Al-Qawāʿid, 1/488.*

[224] Ibn Taymiyyah, *Majmūʿ al-Fatāwa*, 28/68.

Guidelines for Balancing Harms

There are multiple guidelines for balancing between two types of evil, including the following:

1. Preferring Temporary Harm over Lasting One

An example is if a woman migrates from a land of severe persecution or genocide with no *maḥram* to accompany her (which might ordinarily be disallowed in some fiqhi schools of thought). But staying in that land of persecution can be a perpetual evil in some cases, while traveling alone is a temporary harm, so the lesser or shorter evil is chosen. Ibn Taymiyyah cites a similar example and uses the evidence of Umm Kulthūm (rA), for whom the verse ("O you who believe, if believing women come to you as emigrants…")[225] was revealed.[226]

2. Driving Out Greater Harm by Incurring Lesser One

An example of this is praying behind an imam who is openly deviant (in *bidʿah* or immorality). If one truly cannot remove or replace him except through an action that causes a worse harm, it is better to endure this lesser harm by praying behind him. Missing the congregational prayer, Friday prayer, or ʿĪd prayer is a greater harm, so such an imam should still be followed so long as there is no viable alternative[227] – and the community should strive for that.

Among the known fiqhi examples is the following: when wealth endowed for the poor (*māl mawqūf*) exists and several needy persons are present, one of whom is in a state of dire necessity (muḍṭarr), meeting the necessity of that individual is obligatory. If the necessity cannot be relieved except by diminishing the sufficiency (*kifāyah*) allotted to the other poor from the same waqf, without reducing them to necessity, then that reduction becomes compulsory.

Here two harms (*mafsadatān*) arise: the first is the continued hardship of the destitute person, and the second is the diminished sufficiency of the remaining poor. The essential need of the person in dire straits is satisfied, for leaving it unmet constitutes a greater harm than lowering the sufficiency of the others.[228]

---

[225] Qur'an 60:10.
[226] Ibn Taymiyyah, *Majmūʿ al-Fatāwa*, 20/52.
[227] Ibn Taymiyyah, *Majmūʿ al-Fatāwa*, 28/343.
[228] Ibn Taymiyyah, *Majmūʿ al-Fatāwa*, 31/91.

A further illustration of mitigating harm concerns one who aids an oppressed person (*maẓlūm*) by lessening the injustice against him or by paying off the wrongful claim. Such a helper acts as the agent (*wakīl*) of the oppressed, not of the oppressor, comparable to someone who lends him money or undertakes to deliver his funds to the wrongdoer. For example, if a guardian (walī) of an orphan or a waqf is confronted by a tyrant demanding money and, after exhausting all efforts to repel him, satisfies him with a lesser amount, whether paid directly to the tyrant or through an intermediary, he is considered a doer of good (*muḥsin*),[229] and "no blame rests upon those who do good".[230]

Similarly, AI implementation in Muslim contexts frequently requires choosing between competing harms. Facial recognition technology in mosques would present such a dilemma: implementing these systems risks creating surveillance infrastructure that authoritarian regimes could exploit to monitor and persecute Muslims, while refusing such technology may leave communities vulnerable to security threats in an era of rising Islamophobic violence.[231] The harm of potential state surveillance must be weighed against the harm of inadequate security measures. This calculation varies by context; communities in countries with strong civil liberties protections face different risk profiles than those under authoritarian governance. The principle of choosing temporary over permanent harm suggests that, in some countries, security vulnerabilities (or alternatives) might be preferable to establishing permanent surveillance infrastructure that fundamentally alters the mosque's role as a sanctuary.[232]

Digital matchmaking platforms confront Muslim users with unavoidable harm mitigation choices. Providing detailed personal information risks privacy violations, potential stalking, and data exploitation by platform operators, new owners of the company in the event of a sale, or malicious actors. However, maintaining strict privacy limits meaningful connections and may enable deceptive users to misrepresent themselves, potentially leading to harmful interactions. The muwāzanah between privacy harms and connection limitations requires nuanced assessment: temporary privacy compromises for

---

[229] Ibn Taymiyyah, *Majmū' al-Fatāwa*, 28/285.

[230] Qur'an 9:91.

[231] On surveillance in religious spaces, see Howe, Nicolas. "Secular Iconoclasm: Purifying, Privatizing, and Profaning Public Faith." *Social & Cultural Geography* 10, no. 8 (2009): 849-868.

[232] The principle of temporary versus permanent harm derives from the maxim discussed in al-Suyūṭī, Jalāl al-Dīn. *al-Ashbāh wa-al-Naẓā'ir fī Qawā'id wa-Furū' Fiqh al-Shāfi'iyya*. Beirut: Dār al-Kutub al-'Ilmiyya, 1990, 176-184.

specific, verified individuals may be preferable to permanent public exposure, while accepting some communication barriers may prevent greater harms from premature or deceptive emotional attachments.

3. Prioritization Vis-à-vis the Necessities (al-Ḍarūriyyāt)

One of the methods for weighing between harms (*al-mafāsid*) is to give precedence (*tarjīḥ*) according to the levels (*marātib*) of the necessities (*al-ḍarūrīyāt*).

3a. Preserving Religion vs. Preserving Life

The application of fiqh al-muwāzanāt (the jurisprudence of weighing) to conflicts between ḥifẓ al-dīn and ḥifẓ al-nafs represents perhaps the most sophisticated dimension of contemporary Islamic jurisprudential analysis. The principle of "choosing the lesser of two evils" when both fundamental objectives cannot be simultaneously preserved requires a methodological framework that transcends simplistic hierarchical applications.

Building on the works of al-Āmirī (380 H) in the fourth century, al-Ghazālī (d. 505 AH/1111 CE) elaborated on a classification of *maqāṣid* which he placed entirely under what he called 'unrestricted interests' (*al-maṣāliḥ al-mursalah*), although subsequent jurists found themselves grappling with the hierarchical ordering of these fundamental objectives. Fakhr al-Dīn al-Rāzī (d. 606 AH), through *al-Maḥṣūl fī al-ʿIlm al-Uṣūl*, noted that there was a difference in the order of *al-uṣūl al-khamsah* by prioritizing guarding the soul over guarding religion. This divergence from a previous ordering demonstrates the ongoing scholarly debate regarding the relative priority of these essential maqāṣid, particularly during periods when these objectives appear to strongly conflict.

Al-Ghazālī places "the safeguarding of the roots of religion" first because religion secures eternal joy (i.e., paradise), the remaining interests secure only worldly welfare.[233] Al-Shāṭibī later affirms this hierarchy, arguing that without *ḥifẓ al-dīn* the remaining maqāṣid lose their teleological anchor, yet he also concedes that the Sharīʿah occasionally allows a controlled sacrifice of partial religious interests when the very existence of life is threatened.[234] The tension itself is perceived by some jurists to be resolved through two principles: The

---

[233] al-Ghazālī, *al-Mustasfā*, 1:286–88.

[234] al-Shāṭibī, *al-Muwāfaqāt*, 2/8-12.

first is *tartīb al-maqāṣid* (rank-ordering of objectives), which makes ḥifẓ al-dīn categorically weightier than ḥifẓ al-nafs in most cases, but clearly not all. The second is *al-ḍarūrāt tubīḥ al-maḥẓūrāt* ("necessities permit the forbidden"), which authorizes temporary suspension of some religious obligations to avert existential harm. For instance, Allah SWT exempts the believer who utters words of disbelief under duress while his heart remains tranquil with īmān,[235] demonstrating that the sanctity of life can override the outward expression of faith so long as the inward reality of *ḥifẓ al-dīn* endures. Classical jurists therefore distinguish between preserving the *asl* (essence) of religion, which remains inviolable, and preserving its *far'* (secondary manifestations), which may be compromised when death is imminent.

The classical legal maxim, "when two harms conflict, the greater harm is averted by committing the lesser harm" (*idhā ta'āraḍa mafsadatān rū'iya a'ẓamuhumā ḍararan bi-irtikāb akhaffihimā*), establishes the theoretical foundation for contemporary applications. However, the determination of which constitutes the "greater" versus "lesser" evil between religious and vital preservation requires sophisticated jurisprudential analysis that considers multiple contextual factors, the precise issue at hand in a contemporary *fiqh al-muwāzanāt* framework.

In some cases, a multifaceted framework is easier to follow. For instance, in medical emergencies where immediate treatment preserves life but requires actions that temporarily compromise religious observance, the immediacy and certainty of physical harm typically outweighs potential spiritual consequences. However, when religious compromise involves fundamental 'aqīdah (creedal) matters that affect eternal salvation, the calculation becomes more complex.

Second, the scope of impact must be evaluated: whether the consequences affect the individual alone or extend to the broader Muslim community (ummah). The principle of reversibility provides another crucial analytical tool in fiqh al-muwāzanāt applications. This involves assessing whether the chosen course of action allows for future rectification or whether it creates irreversible consequences. Death, being irreversible, often weighs heavily in favor of *ḥifẓ al-nafs*, while many religious compromises can potentially be rectified through subsequent *tawbah* (repentance) and compensation.

[235] Qur'an 16:106.

The COVID-19 pandemic provides compelling contemporary case studies for applying this framework. When health authorities restricted congregational prayers to prevent disease transmission, some argued that *ḥifẓ al-dīn* (protection of religion) is much more important than *ḥifẓ al-nafs* (protection of life). However, sophisticated muwāzanāt analysis reveals that preventing mass casualties serves both maqāṣid simultaneously: preserving life directly serves *ḥifẓ al-nafs*, while maintaining the Muslim community's capacity for future religious practice ultimately serves *ḥifẓ al-dīn*. The temporary suspension of congregational prayer preserves the long-term ability of the community to worship collectively, demonstrating how apparent conflicts can resolve through temporal and consequentialist analysis.

Ibn Taymiyyah synthesizes these doctrines by asserting that the Sharīʿah never commands a harm devoid of benefit, nor prohibits a benefit devoid of harm. Hence, if a believer's life is endangered unless he consumes prohibited food or postpones *ṣalāh*, he must choose life because "the *mafsadah* of immediate destruction outweighs the *mafsadah* of delayed worship."[236] Conversely, if a tyrant demands abjuration of the core tenets of tawḥīd as the price of survival, the believer is obliged to resist, for the extinction of *ḥifẓ al-dīn* itself is the greatest *mafsadah*.[237] In fact, to Ibn Taymiyyah, there exist rare examples of prioritizing *ḥifẓ al-dīn* over *al-nafs* even if it leads to death. He cites the ḥadīth of the People of the Trench,[238] and the story of the boy who allowed himself to be killed so that Islam might prevail,[239] and asserts that safeguarding the faith may override the preservation of one's life in dire, extreme circumstances.[240] He then cited the verse, "persecution/oppression is far worse than killing..."[241] which referred to the case where believers might be attacked either in the sacred months or the sacred mosque, permitting self-defense in this case.[242]

Preserving One Life vs. Another

The classical consensus (*ijmāʿ*) regarding coercion to commit murder provides perhaps the most unambiguous example of *muwāzanāt* application. If a man

---

[236] Ibn Taymiyyah, *Majmūʿ al-Fatāwa*, 20/200.
[237] Ibn ʿĀbidīn, *Radd al-Muḥtār*, 4:262.
[238] The story of the people of the trench is referenced in Sūrah al-Burūj (85).
[239] The story of the boy and the king is found in Sahih Muslim, no. 3005, al-Tirmidhi, no. 3340.
[240] Ibn Taymiyyah, *Majmūʿ al-Fatāwa*, 27/231.
[241] Qur'an 2:217.
[242] Ibn Taymiyyah, *Majmūʿ al-Fatāwa*, 27/231.

is coerced to kill a Muslim or be killed himself, he must not do kill the other individual, by consensus. Preserving his own life is not worth unjustly killing someone else, nor is that any more valid for him than for the other person. This principle establishes that the preservation of innocent life (*ḥifẓ al-nafs*) cannot be achieved through the destruction of equally innocent life. The consensus reflects the fundamental Islamic principle that each soul possesses equal intrinsic value before Allah, and that no individual's right to life supersedes another's equivalent right.

This precedent establishes crucial methodological principles for contemporary applications. First, the principle of numerical equivalence: preservation of life cannot justify the taking of an equal number of innocent lives. Second, the principle of moral agency: coercion mitigates individual culpability but does not eliminate the objective wrongness of the act. Third, the principle of ultimate accountability: the coerced individual remains responsible to Allah for choosing martyrdom over murder, reflecting the supremacy of divine judgment over temporal preservation. These principles find contemporary relevance in scenarios involving medical triage, resource allocation during humanitarian crises, and the pursuit of policies in countries where a policy involves this particular challenge of preserving one life over another.

Preserving Intellect vs. Preserving Life

The permissibility of using wine to dislodge a life-threatening obstruction demonstrates the application of muwāzanāt when preserving life requires temporarily compromising the preservation of intellect. If one is choking and needs wine to dislodge the obstruction, it is permitted to use it, because losing one's life is a greater harm than drinking a small amount of an intoxicant. This ruling reflects the principle that it is not permissible to use intoxicants and other filthy substances as medical treatments, except in cases where the alternatives represent greater harm. The principle rests on several distinctions: the temporary versus permanent nature of intellectual impairment, the certainty of death versus the probability of intoxication, and the minimal quantity required for the medical intervention versus recreational consumption.

Ibn Taymiyyah's stance on not forbidding the Tatars from drinking wine provides a more complex application of this principle, where preventing their sobriety could lead them to far more destructive behavior.[243] So letting them remain partially incapacitated was the lesser harm. This historical example demonstrates contextual muwāzanāt where the standard prohibition against intoxicants was suspended because their psychological and military state when sober posed a greater threat to broader community preservation (*ḥifẓ al-nafs* on a communal scale) than their continued alcohol consumption. Contemporary scholars must exercise extreme caution in applying this precedent, as it operates within the specific historical context of the Mongol invasions and their threat to the very survival of Muslim communities in those regions. The principle nonetheless establishes that preservation of intellect, while fundamentally important, may be temporarily compromised when its preservation would result in greater harm to life and community survival.

In the realm of American political engagement, this principle illuminates the complex calculations facing Muslim voters, organizations, and activists who must navigate between ideological purity and pragmatic effectiveness. The temporary compromise of certain intellectual or religious commitments in exchange for preventing greater societal harm finds expression in strategic political alliances that may require American Muslims to support candidates or policies that do not perfectly align with Islamic principles but prevent more significant damage to Muslim communities or other vulnerable populations.

For instance, supporting political candidates who may have problematic positions on certain moral issues but offer strong protection for religious freedom and minority rights exemplifies this *muwāzanāt* calculation. Contemporary American Muslim organizations frequently employ this reasoning when endorsing candidates who support policies protecting Muslim civil rights and preventing Islamophobic legislation, even when these candidates may hold positions on social issues that conflict with traditional Islamic teachings. The key methodological principle remains that such compromises must be temporary, aimed at preventing greater harm, evaluated through the proposed *fiqh al-muwāzanāt* framework[244] via scholarly councils, and constantly reevaluated as circumstances change.

---

[243] *Al-Istiqāmah*, 277-278.
[244] See Appendix A for full summary.

Preserving Intellect vs. Preserving Property

ʿUmar ibn al-Khaṭṭāb's burning of Ruwayshid al-Thaqafī's wine shop exemplifies prioritizing intellectual preservation over property preservation, providing guidance for American Muslim political advocacy that prioritizes community intellectual and spiritual development over purely economic considerations, supporting policies restricting certain economic activities when they fundamentally undermine community well-being, even when such restrictions negatively impact Muslim-owned businesses.[245]

This principle manifests in supporting regulations on predatory lending, gambling establishments, or exploitative media content targeting vulnerable communities, reflecting prioritization of intellectual and spiritual preservation over short-term economic gains, as exemplified in the 2024-2025 political landscape's unprecedented harm-balancing calculations between candidates who actively support genocide with "progressive" domestic policies versus those combining genocide support with authoritarian domestic agendas, leading some Muslim organizations to strategically withhold endorsements, asserting that legitimizing either option causes greater long-term harm.[246]

The precedent justifies Muslim political support for public education funding, mental health services, and community development programs strengthening intellectual capacity despite higher taxation affecting Muslim business owners, and advocating for zoning restrictions preventing casinos, liquor stores, or "adult" clubs near mosques and schools, arguing that community intellectual and spiritual preservation takes precedence over individual property rights, with ʿUmar's action teaching that political decisions should evaluate long-term community intellectual health rather than immediate economic impact.[247]

During political crises, the harm-balancing framework provides systematic guidance: when facing discriminatory legislation, Muslim organizations must evaluate whether legal challenges, political mobilization, or strategic accommodation best minimizes long-term harm, with the principle of

---

[245] For example, supporting such regulations reflects sophisticated understanding that certain economic activities, while potentially profitable, corrode the intellectual and spiritual fabric of communities.

[246] This contemporary application demonstrates how the classical principle guides navigation of complex political landscapes where all options involve significant moral compromise.

[247] Similarly, this framework includes economic boycotts of businesses or organizations complicit in genocide, occupation (e.g., of Palestine), or oppression, even if potentially harming individual business owners, recognizing that community moral integrity supersedes individual economic interests.

preferring temporary over permanent harm suggesting acceptance of short-term political costs to prevent constitutional precedents creating lasting damage to Muslim civil rights.[248]

4.3. Balancing Between Interests (maṣāliḥ) and Harms (mafāsid)

The third and most intricate category of *fiqh al-muwāzanāt* emerges when scholars and individuals must navigate situations where beneficial and harmful consequences coexist within the same course of action. This category represents perhaps the broadest and most crucial application of muwāzanāt principles, given how frequently these conflicts arise in complex modern contexts. Unlike scenarios where competing benefits or competing harms must be prioritized, this dimension requires the sophisticated evaluation of qualitatively different moral considerations, weighing positive outcomes against negative consequences to determine the overall ethical valuation of a proposed action.

As many scholars note, the frequency and complexity of such calculations intensify during periods of social, political, or religious decline. Such issues multiply in times and places where the marks of prophethood are diminished. The more corruption pervades society, the more complicated these trade-offs become, causing fitnah (trial and discord) among the ummah. Some people focus exclusively on the positive aspects while ignoring negative consequences; others obsess over potential harms while dismissing genuine benefits. True moderation requires comprehensive evaluation of both dimensions, careful assessment of their relative magnitudes, and principled decision-making, though even this process may be compromised if personal desires distort objective judgment.

Revelatory Evidence

The Qur'ānic treatment of wine and gambling provides the paradigmatic example for balancing mixed consequences. Allah says: "They ask you about wine and gambling. Say, 'In them there is great sin and [some] benefit for people. But their sin is greater than their benefit'").[249] This verse establishes several crucial methodological principles for contemporary muwāzanāt applications. First, the Qur'ān explicitly acknowledges that morally

---

[248] This systematic approach ensures that crisis responses are principled rather than reactive, maintaining long-term strategic vision even under immediate pressure.

[249] Qur'an 2:219.

problematic practices may contain genuine benefits, this divine recognition validates the intellectual framework for weighing mixed outcomes rather than demanding absolute categorical thinking. Second, the verse establishes that benefits and harms can be compared and measured against each other, suggesting that moral evaluation requires quantitative as well as qualitative assessment. Third, the Qurʾānic conclusion that "their sin is greater than their benefit" demonstrates that such calculations can yield definitive moral judgments rather than merely theoretical exercises.

The progressive revelation regarding alcohol consumption further illustrates the sophisticated nature of Qurʾānic muwāzanāt. Many scholars note that the verses addressing alcohol were revealed gradually, from initial acknowledgment of both benefits and harms, to prohibition during prayer times, to complete prohibition, suggesting that the balance of benefits and harms may shift depending on community circumstances and spiritual development. This progression provides methodological guidance for contemporary scholars evaluating policies or practices that may serve transitional functions while communities develop toward more ideal arrangements.

Prophetic Precedent

The Prophet's decision regarding rebuilding the Kaʿbah provides perhaps the most instructive example of Prophetic *muwāzanāt* in balancing religious benefits against social harms: he told ʿĀʾishah he would have rebuilt the Kaʿbah upon its original Abrahamic foundation "were it not that your people have recently left disbelief," refraining from restoring the Kaʿbah to its true historical form, though representing a clear *maṣlaḥah*, to avoid the greater *mafsadah* of destabilizing the newly reformed community whose faith remained fragile.[250] This prophetic example demonstrates prioritizing the most important benefit when all benefits cannot be simultaneously achieved.

This Prophetic precedent establishes crucial methodological guidelines: even religiously meritorious actions may be suspended when implementation would cause greater harm to community stability or spiritual development; timing and context significantly affect overall moral calculation where beneficial actions in one circumstance may prove harmful in another; community

[250] Ṣaḥīḥ al-Bukhārī, no. 1585. This decision demonstrates the Prophet's sophisticated understanding of social psychology and community dynamics in religious leadership.

readiness and capacity constitute legitimate factors in pursuing otherwise desirable objectives; and leadership requires wisdom to distinguish between ultimate ideals and immediate practical necessities, with effective governance often requiring graduated approaches toward ideal arrangements.[251]

Artificial intelligence epitomizes technologies where benefits and harms are inextricably intertwined, demanding sophisticated muwāzanah analysis. Large language models democratize access to information, enabling Muslims worldwide to research religious questions, access scholarly texts, and receive personalized guidance. Simultaneously, these systems propagate misinformation, may provide incorrect religious rulings, and potentially diminish the human relationships traditionally central to Islamic knowledge transmission. The calculation cannot simply enumerate benefits versus harms but must evaluate their relative weights: does broadened access to Islamic knowledge outweigh risks of theological confusion? Can technological safeguards minimize harms while preserving benefits? The dynamic nature of AI development means these calculations require constant reassessment as capabilities and risks evolve.

Likewise, digital matchmaking platforms present paradigmatic cases of mixed benefit-harm scenarios requiring careful balancing. Benefits include facilitating marriages for those lacking traditional social networks, enabling connections based on religious compatibility rather than merely cultural similarity, and providing structured communication frameworks that maintain Islamic boundaries. Concurrent harms encompass commodification of marriage decisions, exposure to inappropriate content or interactions, and weakening of community involvement in marriage formation. The *muwāzanah* must consider whether platform modifications can minimize harms while preserving benefits; for instance, requiring *wali* involvement, implementing guardian notifications, ID verification, or establishing waiting periods between initial contact and meeting. The assessment varies based on individual circumstances: platforms may offer net benefits for isolated converts or Muslim minorities while potentially harming those with robust community support who might prematurely bypass traditional channels.

---

251 These four guidelines—suspension of meritorious actions when harmful, contextual timing considerations, community readiness assessment, and graduated implementation—provide a comprehensive framework for contemporary Muslim leaders navigating between religious ideals and practical constraints.

Evidence from Consensus (Ijmāʿ)

The companions' decision-making immediately following the Prophet's death provides compelling evidence for classical consensus on *muwāzanāt* methodology: facing competing religious obligations between the Prophet's immediate burial (a clear religious duty) and establishing caliphal leadership (a crucial political and religious necessity), they determined through collective assessment that selecting a caliph took precedence to preserve community unity and prevent political fragmentation, while burial could be temporarily delayed without fundamental harm, with no Companion objecting to this prioritization, constituting *ijmāʿ* on the legitimacy of weighing competing benefits and choosing the more pressing obligation.[252]

This foundational precedent demonstrates that *muwāzanāt* calculations require collective wisdom rather than individual judgment when possible, with the Companions' consultation process and unanimous agreement suggesting that complex benefit-harm calculations benefit from diverse perspectives and communal discernment, while establishing that religious obligations themselves may be prioritized against each other based on temporal circumstances and community needs rather than operating according to abstract hierarchical arrangements.[253] For contemporary American Muslim political engagement, this precedent supports collective decision-making processes within Muslim organizations and communities when evaluating political candidates, policy positions, or advocacy strategies, suggesting that rather than individual Muslims making isolated calculations about political participation, the Companions' model advocates seeking community consultation and striving for consensus on complex political questions involving weighing religious principles against practical political considerations.[254]

Evidence from Reasoning

The intellectual foundation for *muwāzanāt* rests on both sophisticated jurisprudential reasoning and basic human intuitive capacity for preferential judgment. As Ibn Taymiyyah notes throughout his writings on these topics, it

---

[252] This historical moment represents perhaps the most significant collective *muwāzanāt* decision in Islamic history, establishing precedent for prioritizing community preservation even over immediate religious obligations.

[253] The principle that even clear religious duties can be temporarily postponed for greater communal benefit revolutionizes understanding of Islamic legal flexibility in crisis situations.

[254] This collective approach ensures that political decisions reflect community wisdom and shared responsibility rather than individual preferences or isolated interpretations.

is known to any rational individual that prioritizing the most preponderant of interests over those less so is praiseworthy and good, and that averting the most harmful of harms is praiseworthy and good. This rational foundation extends beyond learned scholars to encompass basic human decision-making capacity. Even children naturally choose more beneficial over less beneficial options when presented with clear alternatives, such as selecting more delicious over less delicious food, or valuable over less valuable objects.

This intuitive capacity suggests that muwāzanāt calculations, while requiring scholarly expertise for complex applications, operate according to principles accessible to ordinary Muslims facing everyday decisions. The rational foundation also implies that muwāzanāt methodology can be communicated and taught to Muslim communities, enabling broader participation in complex moral reasoning rather than restricting such calculations to private councils.

When benefits and harms coexist within proposed actions, Ibn Taymiyyah provides crucial methodological guidance: When two obligations compete and cannot be fulfilled together, the more important takes precedence, and the lesser one is no longer obligatory in this situation. The person who abandons the lesser obligation to fulfill the more important one is not, in reality, abandoning an obligation. If one cannot realize a strongly recommended virtue (*ḥasanah rājihah*) except by committing a smaller vice, and there is no way around it, then that "vice" effectively becomes permissible or even obligatory in that context. By analogy, *eating a dead animal (maytah)* in times of necessity is allowed, or *wearing silk* in freezing temperatures. Some individuals hesitate to do this, only focusing on the wrongdoing aspect, failing to see the greater good or essential need.[255]

This principle extends to situations involving benefits and harms: actions that ordinarily would be prohibited may become permissible or even required when they serve greater beneficial purposes, while normally beneficial actions may be restricted when they produce disproportionate harm.

As Ibn Taymiyyah notes, the Sharīʿah's treatment of warfare,[256] with conditions, exemplifies this principle.[257] Despite the obvious harms associated

[255] Ibn Taymiyyah, *Majmūʿ al-Fatāwa*, 35/29.
[256] Qur'an 2:216.
[257] Ibn Taymiyyah, *Majmūʿ al-Fatāwa*, 11/623.

with combat, the Qur'ān prescribes fighting when it yields net benefits for society, such as when protecting them from invasions, occupations, and general attacks on their lives and families. Conversely, wine and gambling are prohibited despite containing some benefits, because their harms predominate. This divine precedent establishes that moral evaluation must consider total consequences rather than isolated aspects of actions.

Conversely, certain things normally obligatory or praiseworthy might become forbidden or discouraged if they yield a worse consequence. Examples include a sick person harming himself by fasting, or using water for wuḍū' if it endangers life, etc. One day, a companion who was injured badly was told by others that he must still perform wuḍū' instead of tayammum, and the man died because of it. The Prophet ﷺ famously said: *"They killed him; may God kill them! Why did they not ask if they did not know? Indeed, the cure for ignorance is to ask."*[258]

As Ibn Taymiyyah notes, the category of fulfilling obligations is greater than the category of avoiding prohibitions, and the category of neglecting obligations is graver than the category of committing prohibitions.[259] He supported this with over thirty evidences, including:

- The greatest of good deeds is belief in Allah and His Messenger, and belief is a positive, affirmative act.
- The five pillars of Islam are of the category of obligations, and there has been disagreement regarding the disbelief of one who abandons them. However, none of the scholars from Ahl al-Sunnah have declared disbelief for committing prohibitions unless such acts contradict faith.
- The sin of Iblīs was abandoning an obligation, which was prostration, while the sin of Ādam was a prohibition, which was eating from the tree. Thus, the sin of Iblīs was greater and preceded that of Ādam.
- Good deeds, which consist of fulfilling obligations, erase the punishment of sins and misdeeds that involve committing prohibitions. As for good deeds, bad deeds do not erase their reward at all.
- Performing good deeds necessitates abandoning sinful acts, whereas merely refraining from sinful acts does not necessitate performing good deeds. Thus, performing good deeds encompasses both aspects, making it more virtuous and superior.

---

[258] Sunan Abū Dāwūd, no. 336.

[259] *Majmū' al-Fatāwā*, Ibn Taymiyyah, 20:85.

4.4. Contemporary Applications to Political Strategy

Electoral Participation Calculations

Muslim American electoral participation exemplifies complex benefit-harm balancing. Engaging in democratic processes offers benefits of civic representation, policy influence, and community protection, while potentially involving compromises with corrupted systems or candidates. The framework enables systematic evaluation: when democratic participation's benefits (protecting Muslim civil rights, advancing social justice, preventing greater harms through political marginalization) substantially outweigh its costs (association with imperfect political systems), engagement becomes not merely permissible but recommended.

Coalition Building Analysis

When Muslim organizations consider joining coalitions for religious freedom, civil rights, or social justice, muwāzanāt methodology provides evaluation criteria. Benefits include amplified political influence, shared resources, and broader social acceptance. Potential harms involve association with groups holding conflicting positions on other significant issues or dilution of distinctly Islamic messaging. The key consideration remains whether coalition participation enhances Muslim capacity to achieve legitimate objectives while maintaining religious integrity.

Post-October 2023 coalition dynamics require muwāzanāt applications as Muslim organizations navigate between maintaining necessary alliances while avoiding complicity in genocide normalization. When longtime coalition partners enforce litmus tests requiring silence on Palestinian rights, the framework evaluates whether temporary coalition dissolution better serves long-term justice objectives than compromised participation.

Policy Advocacy Prioritization

Muslim American organizations face constant decisions about resource allocation across competing policy priorities. Systematic muwāzanāt enables strategic evaluation: immigration reform might offer substantial benefits for Muslim communities while requiring cooperation with groups holding problematic positions on other issues. Environmental protection initiatives may align with Islamic stewardship principles while necessitating alliances with secular environmental movements. The methodology provides frameworks for evaluating such mixed scenarios systematically rather than through ad hoc decision-making.

It should be noted clearly that approaches to muwāzanah on complex issues do not always follow one order as the five conditions above, nor are they fixed to these five conditions in all scenarios. Take for instance the case study of artificial intelligence, with a request for iftāʾ on a particular angle of daily-use AI. An approach that integrates the five conditions above pre-muwāzanah would likely follow this methodology:

1. The ruling must begin with accurate conceptualization, not with the label "AI." The first task is *taṣwīr al-masʾalah*: identifying the precise act, context, user, system function, affected parties, representations made, rights implicated, and probable harms or benefits. "Using AI" is not a single legal category.
2. General principles must be attached to the specific case through *taḥqīq al-manāṭ*. A jurist must determine whether the relevant legal description actually applies. The same tool may function as assistance, deception, impersonation, surveillance, emotional manipulation, fraud, or harmless convenience depending on use and context.
3. The baseline ruling for worldly tools is permissibility, but this default is conditional. AI as a technical means is not prohibited merely because it is new. However, permissibility may be altered by unlawful content, intention, deception, rights violations, foreseeable harm, or use as a means to the unlawful.
4. The analysis must distinguish between *taklīfī* and *waḍʿī* rulings. An act may be sinful without automatically invalidating a contract, grade, certificate, marriage claim, or evidentiary process. Moral responsibility, legal validity, liability, and enforceable consequences require distinct analysis.
5. *Fiqh al-wāqiʿ* is indispensable. A sound ruling requires a disciplined understanding of what the technology actually does, what it cannot do, how reliable it is, how users interact with it, and what risks are known. Marketing claims, public fear, and exaggerated assumptions should not substitute for reality.
6. *Maqāṣid* and *qawāʿid* must guide the analysis while remaining anchored in the sources. The preservation of religion, intellect, family, property, dignity, privacy, reputation, and public trust is directly relevant to AI. These objectives must be applied through concrete juristic categories such as *ghish*, *tadlīs*, *tajassus*, *qadhf*-like

reputational harm, *shahādat al-zūr*, *amānah*, *ta'āwun 'alā al-ithm*, and *ḍamān*.

7. Consequences must be considered, especially where AI harms emerge through scale and repetition. I'tibār al-ma'ālāt is essential because many AI uses appear minor in isolation but become harmful through personalization, normalization, emotional dependency, reputational virality, institutional reliance, or gradual erosion of discipline and truthfulness.
8. *Sadd al-dharā'i'* must be applied with proportionality. Blocking the means is justified where a use is likely to lead to serious harm, such as sexualized AI companionship, nonconsensual likeness generation, religious deepfakes, deceptive authorship, or systems designed to drive users toward unlawful content. It should not be invoked loosely against beneficial, bounded, transparent uses.
9. Benefits and harms must be ranked through *awlawiyyāt* and *muwāzanāt*. Not every concern carries the same legal weight. Definite harms are not equal to speculative harms; public harms are not equal to private inconvenience; harms to children, religion, family, reputation, and public trust require greater caution; and benefits must be weighed against both immediate and long-term harms.
10. The final ruling must be applied with precision, humility, and proper institutional distinction. *Tanzīl al-ḥukm* requires applying the ruling to the case with its conditions, limits, and degree of certainty. The analysis must also distinguish between personal sin, fatwa, institutional policy, and judicial ruling. A Muslim school, masjid, employer, mufti, arbitrator, and court may each address the same AI-related act through different standards because their functions, evidentiary thresholds, and responsibilities differ.

Taken together, these principles demonstrate that the fiqh of daily-use AI cannot be reduced to a single permissive or prohibitive posture. The Sharī'ah-based approach is neither technophobic nor naïve. It recognizes AI as a powerful set of means whose rulings vary according to purpose, content, disclosure, rights, consequences, and institutional context. A credible Islamic treatment must therefore preserve the revealed moral order while engaging the actual conditions of contemporary technological life with clarity, restraint, and juristic seriousness.

5

Strategic Principles for Implementation

While the previous chapters established the essential conditions and typologies for Islamic legal balancing, this chapter demonstrates their application through three contemporary case studies: Muslim political participation in Western democracies, the governance of artificial intelligence technologies, and the navigation of digital matchmaking platforms. These domains exemplify scenarios where Muslims face unprecedented challenges requiring sophisticated balancing between competing interests, benefits, and harms—situations where pure Islamic ideals must engage with complex realities that offer no perfect solutions. The following strategic principles emerge from applying muwāzanāt methodology to these contemporary challenges, revealing how classical Islamic jurisprudential wisdom provides actionable guidance for Muslims navigating modernity's ethical complexities while maintaining religious integrity and advancing community welfare.

5.1. The Principle of Temporal Urgency

Within American Muslim political engagement, temporal considerations assume critical importance. Legislative windows, electoral cycles, and policy debates operate within compressed timeframes that rarely accommodate extended scholarly deliberation. The principle that preventing harm takes precedence over securing benefits (*dar' al-mafāsid muqaddam ʿalā jalb al-maṣāliḥ*) suggests that providing immediate guidance based on established principles may be preferable to prolonged deliberation allowing preventable harms to multiply.[260] American Muslim communities frequently face political developments where scholarly silence can result in exponentially increasing

[260] When Muslim students face discriminatory policies, when mosques encounter zoning restrictions, or when Muslim candidates seek community support, the temporal element becomes crucial to effective muwāzanāt.

mafāsid. When immigration policies threaten family unity or educational policies impact Islamic identity formation, the absence of timely scholarly direction leaves community members navigating challenges without proper sharīʿah-based frameworks.[261]

The methodology of strategic gradualism emerges as paramount for navigating complex political transformations, with the Qur'ānic paradigm establishing gradualism as fundamental to divine pedagogy through the twenty-three-year revelation process demonstrating that even perfect divine guidance was transmitted through carefully calibrated stages.[262] ʿUmar ibn ʿAbd al-ʿAzīz responded to his son's impatience with reform: "Do not be in such haste. God condemned wine twice in the Qur'ān, and then prohibited it the third time. I am afraid of imposing the truth on the people all at once for they will reject it all at once, and this will lead to trial."

This response reveals profound jurisprudential insight establishing that divine wisdom employs gradualism, comprehensive rejection results from precipitous implementation, sustainable change requires alignment between external requirements and internal capacity, and prudential leadership involves managing transformation tempo.[263]

Gradualism's primary objectives include systematic alleviation of hardship while preventing social discord (*fitnah*), positioning it as an essential mechanism within comprehensive legal balancing that functions as applied wisdom (*ḥikmah*), harmonizing divine objectives with human capacity while simultaneously opening pathways to benefit (*fatḥ al-dharāʾiʿ*) and blocking routes to harm (*sadd al-dharāʾiʿ*).[264]

The Prophet's instructions to Muʿādh regarding Yemen demonstrate systematic gradualism through sequential priority establishment, conditional progression, sensitivity to capacity, and strategic patience, though in the Muslim American political context, accelerating authoritarian drift and

---

[261] Organizations at national or regional levels should consider a time-based framework for responding to urgent situations requiring balancing of interests and harms.

[262] This temporal methodology reflects not limitation but wisdom: recognition that human societies require progressive adaptation to absorb and implement transformative principles effectively.

[263] ʿUmar ibn ʿAbd al-ʿAzīz's son ʿAbd al-Malik had declared willingness to endure any consequence "if in matters of truth the pots begin to boil between you and me," revealing the natural human tendency toward impatience that necessitates deliberate cultivation of measured restraint.

[264] Mohammad Hashim Kamali, *Principles of Islamic Jurisprudence* (Cambridge: Islamic Texts Society, 2003). This dual function—facilitating beneficial change while preventing destructive disruption—creates optimal conditions for sustainable transformation.

systematic targeting of Palestinian advocacy since 2023, including congressional attempts to codify IHRA definitions criminalizing legitimate political speech, may require recalibrating gradualist approaches when institutional capture accelerates faster than community capacity building, necessitating *muwāzanāt* calculations weighing whether continued gradualism risks permanent structural exclusion against dangers of precipitous action.[265]

Similarly, the exponential pace of AI development exemplifies contexts where temporal urgency modifies traditional gradualist approaches. While classical Islamic reform proceeded across generations, AI capabilities double approximately every six months, with systems achieving competencies that fundamentally reshape human activities before communities can develop considered responses. The principle of preventing escalating harm suggests that Muslim communities cannot afford extended deliberation periods when AI systems are actively deployed in ways affecting Muslim lives—from biased hiring algorithms to automated content moderation censoring Islamic content. Strategic interventions must occur during narrow windows when technologies remain malleable rather than after harmful implementations become entrenched industry standards.

Digital matchmaking platforms likewise demonstrate how technological adoption patterns create urgency in religious guidance. These platforms experience network effects where value increases with user adoption, creating tipping points after which they become primary venues for Muslim matrimonial searches.[266] Delayed scholarly engagement allows platform norms to solidify around potentially problematic practices, including anonymous browsing without identification verification, appearance-based filtering, casual communication patterns. These practices become increasingly difficult to modify once user expectations establish. The window for shaping platform development toward Islamic values narrows rapidly as venture capital pressures push toward engagement maximization over matrimonial

[265] The Prophet's instructions involved beginning with fundamental theological concepts before procedural obligations, advancing only after achieving acceptance of prior stages, recognizing that overwhelming populations with comprehensive obligations simultaneously may result in total rejection, and accepting temporary incomplete implementation to secure long-term comprehensive adoption.

[266] Network effects in platform economies are analyzed in Parker, Geoffrey G., Marshall W. Van Alstyne, and Sangeet Paul Choudary. *Platform Revolution*. New York: W. W. Norton, 2016.

success, suggesting that principled intervention during early adoption phases carries disproportionate influence over long-term community practices.[267]

5.2. Balancing Goals (ghāyāt) and Means (wasā'il) in Democratic Participation

The classical principle of balancing between ultimate objectives and instrumental mechanisms proves essential for Muslim American political engagement. The *ghāyah* encompasses protection and advancement of ethical values, Muslim community welfare, social justice promotion, and fulfillment of the witnessing role.[268] The *wasā'il* represents various democratic mechanisms: voting, coalition-building, advocacy, lobbying, and electoral participation.

Contemporary Muslim American political discourse reveals concerning patterns of means-ends confusion, where political parties and policy positions become ends in themselves rather than instruments toward broader Islamic objectives. The notion that the means (*wasīlah*) is nearness requires constant reevaluation of political strategies based on their effectiveness in achieving legitimate ethical objectives.[269]

The Prophetic model provides instructive precedents. The Treaty of Ḥudaybiyyah exemplifies sophisticated political calculation prioritizing long-term strategic objectives over immediate tactical preferences.[270] 'Umar ibn al-Khaṭṭāb's administrative innovations demonstrate institutional adaptation in service of Islamic governance, prioritizing effective administration over rigid adherence to pre-existing political forms.[271] Contemporary manifestations include Muslim organizations developing parallel institutional structures when mainstream political channels prove systematically compromised. The

---

[267] The window for influencing platform development reflects the path dependency discussed in a technologically older publication in Arthur, W. Brian. "Competing Technologies, Increasing Returns, and Lock-In by Historical Events." *The Economic Journal* 99, no. 394 (1989): 116-131.

[268] These goals align with the Quranic injunction: "And thus We have made you a justly balanced community that you will be witnesses over the people" (al-Baqarah: 143), establishing Muslim engagement's fundamental purpose as constructive participation and moral leadership. See Muḥammad ibn Jarīr al-Ṭabarī, *Jāmi' al-Bayān fī Ta'wīl al-Qur'ān*, ed. Aḥmad Muḥammad Shākir (Beirut: Mu'assasat al-Risālah, 2000), 3:142-156.

[269] Muḥammad ibn Aḥmad al-Qurṭubī, *Al-Jāmi' li-Aḥkām al-Qur'ān* (Beirut: Dār al-Kutub al-'Ilmiyyah, 1996), 6:159.

[270] For detailed analysis of the Treaty of Ḥudaybiyyah, see Muḥammad Ḥamīdullāh, *Majmū'at al-Wathā'iq al-Siyāsiyyah* (Beirut: Dār al-Nafā'is, 1987), 56-78.

[271] On 'Umar's administrative innovations, see 'Abd al-'Azīz al-Dūrī, Al-Nuẓum al-Islāmiyyah (Beirut: Markaz Dirāsāt al-Waḥdah al-'Arabiyyah, 1993), 89-112.

creation of alternative media platforms,[272] independent political action committees refusing pro-Israel lobby funding, and grassroots organizing networks outside traditional party structures exemplifies the principle that when existing structures become irredeemably corrupt, building new foundations becomes not merely permissible but obligatory.[273]

AI development illustrates the critical distinction between legitimate goals and questionable means in Islamic engagement with transformative technologies. The *ghāyah* of benefiting humanity through enhanced capabilities, such as medical diagnosis, educational access, and economic efficiency, aligns with Islamic objectives of human flourishing. However, the *wasā'il* of achieving these benefits through systems trained on improperly obtained data, deployed without transparency, or designed to manipulate human behavior contradicts Islamic ethical principles.[274] Muslim technologists face choices between participating in AI development that advances beneficial capabilities while compromising on ethical means, versus developing alternative frameworks that may achieve less immediate impact but maintain principled approaches. The framework suggests that means fundamentally shape outcomes; in other words, AI systems built on exploitative foundations will perpetuate exploitation regardless of stated beneficial intentions.

Digital matchmaking platforms reveal how means can subvert goals when commercial imperatives override religious objectives. While the stated *ghāyah* involves facilitating Islamic marriages, platform *wasā'il* often contradict this purpose: engagement-maximizing algorithms that promote endless browsing over commitment, premium features that create economic barriers to marriage, and interface designs borrowed from casual dating applications that encourage superficial evaluation.[275]

The muwāzanah framework indicates that Muslims should either demand fundamental restructuring of platform mechanisms to align with matrimonial goals or develop alternative systems where means and ends achieve

---

[272] Zeteo, the platform created by journalist Mehdi Hasan, is an example of an independent media platform that is not reliant on Zionist lobbying, wealthy donors, or western or eastern government influences, while of course it is not intended to be a religious media platform for Muslims.

[273] Similar ideas are expressed by Ibn Khaldun about civilizational changes; see Ibn Khaldun, *Muqaddimah*, trans. Franz Rosenthal (Princeton: Princeton University Press, 1967).

[274] On discussions surrounding ethical AI development, see Dignum, Virginia. *Responsible Artificial Intelligence: How to Develop and Use AI in a Responsible Way*. Cham: Springer, 2019.

[275] The commercialization of intimacy is analyzed in Illouz, Eva. *Cold Intimacies: The Making of Emotional Capitalism*. Cambridge: Polity Press, 2007.

consistency. Accepting platforms that nominally serve Muslim audiences while employing means antithetical to Islamic marriage principles represents a category error that confuses accessibility with acceptability.

5.3. The Jurisprudence of Lesser Harm

Classical frameworks for navigating situations where perfect Islamic solutions are unavailable prove particularly relevant to democratic engagement, where pure options rarely exist and political participation often requires choosing between imperfect alternatives.[276] The application of choosing the lesser of two harms recognizes that supporting candidates aligning with some Islamic values while contradicting others may represent legitimate strategic choice when alternatives present greater harm to Muslim interests. However, such flexibility requires clear ethical boundaries. The classical concept that necessities permit prohibitions (*ḍarūrāt tubīḥ al-maḥẓūrāt*) applies only within strict limits, requiring that any compromise be proportionate to necessity, temporary in nature, and aimed at preventing greater harm.[277]

The integration of AI into essential services creates scenarios where complete avoidance becomes practically impossible, necessitating sophisticated application of lesser harm principles. Muslims requiring medical care increasingly encounter AI-diagnostic systems, job seekers face AI-screening processes, and students engage AI-powered educational platforms. Absolute withdrawal would result in exclusion from healthcare, employment, and education, harms exceeding those from cautious engagement.

The framework suggests principled interaction strategies: using AI medical tools while maintaining human physician oversight, engaging AI hiring systems while developing parallel referral networks, and utilizing educational AI while preserving traditional mentorship relationships. These approaches acknowledge technological reality while minimizing harm through conscious limitation and complementary traditional practices.

Similarly, digital matchmaking platforms exemplify contexts requiring nuanced application of lesser harm jurisprudence. For Muslims in geographic isolation, with limited community connections, or facing family dysfunction, these platforms may represent the most viable path toward marriage, an

---

276 ʿIzz al-Dīn ibn ʿAbd al-Salām, *Qawāʿid al-Aḥkām*, 1:61-85.

277 For the principle of necessity in Islamic law, see Wahbah al-Zuḥaylī, *Al-Fiqh al-Islāmī wa-Adillatuh* (Damascus: Dār al-Fikr, 1997), 1:89-123.

essential Islamic objective. Complete avoidance could result in prolonged unmarried status with associated spiritual and social challenges. The lesser harm framework suggests structured engagement protocols: time-limited platform use with clear intentions, involvement of trusted advisors despite platform anonymity features, and transition to conventional communication channels once initial connections establish. Such approaches recognize platform limitations while pragmatically pursuing legitimate objectives, treating digital tools as temporary bridges rather than permanent residences.

5.4. Balancing Strategic Coherence and Community Mobilization

Implementing *fiqh al-muwāzanāt* requires systematic coordination between scholarly analysis and community mobilization to avoid fragmentation weakening Muslim political effectiveness, addressing the gap between theoretical frameworks and practical implementation through organized community action while recognizing that sustainable political engagement depends upon institutional capacity rather than ad hoc responses.[278]

Effective application demands institutional infrastructure bridging scholarly deliberation with grassroots mobilization, with al-Shāṭibī's emphasis on qualified interpretation (*ijtihād*) in contemporary applications establishing that complex political balancing requires specialized competency rather than popular consensus.[279] This involves establishing Qualified Council Requirements ensuring bodies applying this methodology include scholars demonstrating mastery of *maqāṣid* methodology and balancing principles, contextual experts in American political systems and constitutional law, and community representatives who can articulate practical implementation challenges and assess real-world consequences.[280]

The principle that rulings follow their underlying reasons in presence and absence requires institutional mechanisms capable of analyzing contemporary political contexts through established Islamic legal reasoning rather than superficial analogies, necessitating ongoing scholarly development in

---

278 On the necessity of institutional frameworks for effective Islamic governance, see 'Abd al-Wahhāb Khallāf, *'Ilm Uṣūl al-Fiqh* (Cairo: Maktabat al-Da'wah al-Islāmiyyah, 1990).

279 Abū Isḥāq al-Shāṭibī, *Al-I'tiṣām* (Riyadh: Dār Ibn 'Affān, 1997), 2:178-201. This principle prevents the dilution of sophisticated jurisprudential reasoning through uninformed popular opinion.

280 The three-component structure ensures comprehensive analysis combining theoretical expertise, practical knowledge, and community perspectives.

American *fiqh* addressing particular challenges of minority Muslim political participation within secular democratic frameworks.[281]

Documentation and Methodological Consistency

The requirement for systematic documentation emerges from classical emphasis on preserving reasoning processes (*taʿlīl*) underlying legal determinations, with Ibn Taymiyyah's insistence that Islamic governance must demonstrate both divine adherence and practical effectiveness establishing accountability as integral to legitimate authority.[282] This creates institutional responsibility for systematic recording of reasoning processes documenting specific balancing considerations, textual evidence, and contextual analysis; outcome evaluation systems comparing predicted versus actual consequences to refine methodological application; and institutional memory development creating accessible repositories of precedents and lessons learned.[283]

Contemporary scholars like Dr. al-Qaraḍāwī emphasize that *fiqh al-wāqiʿ* (jurisprudence of reality) requires continuous engagement with changing circumstances rather than static application of inherited precedents, demanding institutional frameworks capable of systematic learning and methodological refinement based on practical experience in American political contexts.[284]

The challenge of AI governance demonstrates why strategic coherence requires unprecedented coordination between Islamic scholars, technical experts, and affected communities. Individual Muslims making isolated decisions about AI use cannot adequately address systemic challenges requiring collective response. Effective muwāzanah demands institutional frameworks connecting those who understand AI's architecture with scholars capable of *fiqhi* analysis and communities experiencing direct impact. This tripartite engagement model prevents both naive technological determinism and disconnected theoretical pronouncements, enabling responses that reflect genuine understanding of both Islamic principles and technological realities.

---

[281] Jalāl al-Dīn al-Suyūṭī, *Al-Ashbāh wa-l-Naẓāʾir* (Beirut: Dār al-Kutub al-'Ilmiyyah, 1990), 1:45. This ongoing development recognizes that American Muslim political engagement presents unique challenges requiring contextualized jurisprudential responses.

[282] This classical foundation establishes that transparency and accountability are not modern impositions but intrinsic to Islamic governance methodology.

[283] These three components—documentation, evaluation, and institutional memory—create a learning system that improves over time rather than repeating errors.

[284] This dynamic approach recognizes that American political contexts present unique challenges requiring continuous methodological adaptation while maintaining principled consistency.

Digital matchmaking platforms illustrate how absence of coordinated community response leads to fragmented individual negotiations with powerful systems. When each user independently navigates platform challenges, including privacy settings, communication boundaries, and profile representations, some platforms extract maximum data while providing minimal accountability.[285] Strategic coherence requires collective bargaining approaches: communities establishing shared standards for platform engagement, creating accountability mechanisms for user behavior, and potentially developing community-owned alternatives that embed Islamic values in technological architecture rather than retrofitting secular systems. Such coordination transforms Muslims from passive consumers into active shapers of digital environments affecting fundamental life decisions.[286]

Community Education and Leadership Development

Long-term success of principled political engagement requires systematic community education developing widespread understanding of balancing methodologies, with al-ʿAlwānī emphasizing that contemporary *ijtihād* requires both traditional Islamic scholarship and modern disciplines.[287] This necessitates comprehensive curricula integrating Islamic and American political knowledge, mentorship programs following the Prophet's graduated responsibility model, and communication networks enabling timely guidance through genuine *shūrā* mechanisms.[288] Post-2023 priorities must include digital security as Islamic knowledge, given how pro-Israel organizations

---

[285] On platform power dynamics, see Gillespie, Tarleton. *Custodians of the Internet: Platforms, Content Moderation, and the Hidden Decisions That Shape Social Media*. New Haven: Yale University Press, 2018.

[286] Community ownership models are explored in Scholz, Trebor. *Platform Cooperativism: Challenging the Corporate Sharing Economy*. New York: Rosa Luxemburg Stiftung, 2016. For Islamic frameworks, see Ayub, Muhammad. *Understanding Islamic Finance*. Chichester: John Wiley & Sons, 2007, especially discussions of mushārakah and community-based models.

[287] Ṭāhā Jābir al-ʿAlwānī's work on Islamic methodology establishes this dual requirement, challenging traditional educational models that separate Islamic sciences from contemporary disciplines. Educational curricula must teach both Islamic political theory and American constitutional principles, enabling community members to understand reasoning behind scholarly guidance rather than merely accepting conclusions, addressing classical Islamic sciences alongside American political science, constitutional law, and policy analysis.

[288] Mentorship and leadership pipeline development must link experienced practitioners with emerging leaders through structured programs combining theoretical learning with practical political experience. The Prophet's method of preparing companions for leadership responsibilities through graduated responsibility and continuous guidance provides the paradigmatic model. Communication networks and rapid response systems must enable timely dissemination of guidance during critical political moments while maintaining methodological rigor, with the classical concept of *shūrā* (consultation) requiring institutional mechanisms that facilitate genuine deliberation rather than mere ratification of predetermined positions.

weaponize data against Muslim activists, making encryption and surveillance resistance part of preserving legitimate political expression.[289]

Integration with Broader Islamic Institutional Development

Strategic coherence requires recognizing political engagement within broader Islamic institutional development in America, where effective participation depends upon authentic community identity rooted in Islamic scholarship rather than reactive responses to external pressures.[290] This necessitates coordinating political engagement with institutions producing scholars versed in both Islamic tradition and American contexts, community service organizations demonstrating values through practical benefit rather than mere advocacy, and conditional multi-faith relationship building establishing Muslims as constructive contributors rather than special interest groups.[291] The objective remains maximizing Muslim capacity to advance Islamic values and societal welfare through sophisticated understanding honoring both Islamic universality and American political particularity, requiring institutional sophistication matching democratic complexity while maintaining principled foundations.[292]

[289] Teaching encryption, secure communication, and doxxing prevention becomes part of preserving the community's ability to engage in legitimate political expression. This contemporary addition recognizes that digital surveillance and doxxing campaigns have become primary tools for suppressing Muslim political participation, making digital security a religious obligation for community preservation equivalent to protecting physical safety.

[290] As emphasized by diverse Muslim American scholars for decades, community identity must be perceived in its true diversity, with authentic identity formation preceding effective political engagement to avoid reactive or assimilationist approaches.

[291] These three coordinated areas ensure political engagement emerges from strong community foundations rather than operating in isolation. Educational institution development must produce scholars capable of sophisticated engagement with both traditions; community service must demonstrate Islamic values through tangible social benefit; and civic relationships must be built with clear conditions that preserve Islamic principles while engaging constructively.

[292] This mature understanding of political engagement requires institutional sophistication that matches the complexity of democratic participation while maintaining clear connection to Islamic foundational principles, representing the practical application of *fiqh al-muwāzanāt* to American Muslim political engagement.

6

When Muwāzanah Reaches Its Limits

Despite sophisticated *fiqh al-muwāzanāt* methodology, scholars may encounter situations where systematic interest-balancing proves insufficient, with exhaustive application of the five conditions, three balancing methodologies, and temporal strategies yielding inconclusive results where benefits and detriments appear genuinely equivalent.[293] Classical Islamic jurisprudence anticipated such limitations, developing three complementary approaches representing not methodological failures but recognition that certain decisions transcend rational analysis alone, offering structured approaches when traditional *muwāzanāt* cannot definitively resolve competing considerations between Islamic principles and contemporary issues.

It is crucial for scholars and the laymen to remember that the balancing process is neither purely rational nor purely spiritual. Rather, it is a composite act that integrates evidence, deliberation, consultation, sincerity, and supplication. Among the instruments that strengthen this process are istishārah (consultation) and istikhārah (seeking divine guidance).

These two tools are not marginal devotional acts but essential elements of a juristic methodology that aims to preserve the integrity of the law and the welfare of the community. *Istishārah* ensures breadth of perspective through engagement with qualified voices, while *istikhārah* ensures that the process remains anchored in divine wisdom beyond human calculation. When woven into the jurist's balancing act, these instruments provide clarity at moments of uncertainty and humility at moments of confidence.

---

[293] These situations particularly arise when all major political candidates support fundamental violations of Islamic ethics while differing only in degree, making traditional cost-benefit analysis insufficient and necessitating enhanced reliance on divine guidance and collective wisdom beyond pure rational calculation.

This chapter explores their role in *fiqh al-muwāzanāt* with a focus on second-level consultation. In Chapter 4, the balancing process included an initial *istishārah*, in which scholars and specialists weighed the potential *maṣāliḥ* and *mafāsid* in the area of fiqh al-wāqiʿ. Yet in some cases, after this process is completed, councils still find themselves at an impasse. The competing considerations may appear nearly equal, or the possible outcomes may remain opaque. At that point, the juristic process requires a second-level turn to *istishārah* and *istikhārah*, not as repetition, but as deepening. This "round two" reflects the humility to acknowledge that the first balancing did not resolve the matter and that further avenues of wisdom must be pursued.

6.1. Second-Level Istishārah: Consultation after Impasse

Istishārah in its first layer is an obligatory safeguard against insularity. It ensures that the weighing of *maṣlaḥah* and *mafsadah* is not conducted in a vacuum but is informed by those with insight into the relevant realities. However, when a scholarly council has already carried out such consultation and the deliberation still yields no clear resolution, the second level of *istishārah* emerges.

This form of consultation is more focused, more urgent, and often more specialized. The council recognizes that the usual tools of jurisprudence have reached their limit. At this point, the purpose of *istishārah* is not merely to gather perspectives, but to test the strength of competing arguments once more, to invite scrutiny from voices that were not present in the first round, or to subject the council's reasoning to external critique. Al-Nawawī (rA) said: It is recommended that one consult, before the istikhārah, someone whose condition is known for sincerity, compassion, and experience, and who is trusted for his religion and knowledge. Allah, Exalted is He, said: '…and consult them in the affair.'[294] If he consults, and it becomes apparent that it is in his interest, then he should seek guidance from Allah, Exalted is He, concerning it. In a second-level context, this may involve consulting experts outside the immediate scholarly circle who were consulted the first time, such as additional specialists in technology, sociology, or political science, depending on the issue at hand.

[294] Qur'an 3:159.

Ibn Taymiyyah famously remarked that no one regrets combining *istishārah* of the creation with *istikhārah* of the Creator.[295] This statement is particularly relevant when the council faces deadlock. The second-level *istishārah* becomes an act of institutional humility, signaling to the community that their leaders do not force premature closure when clarity has not yet emerged. Rather, they expand the circle of wisdom, demonstrating that the pursuit of the right balance is itself an act of worship and stewardship.

Prophetic precedents including military strategy, diplomatic treaties, and community governance, and the Quranic principle emphasizing consultation as characteristic of righteous communities: "whose affair is [determined by] consultation among themselves."[296] Contemporary application requires engagement with individuals possessing relevant expertise (*ahl al-khibrah*) rather than general opinion, necessitating scholars with both Islamic legal expertise and practical understanding of American political systems

6.2. Second Alternative: Seeking Divine Guidance through Prayer (Istikhārah)

Istikhārah represents systematic divine guidance-seeking through prayer when human analytical capacity reaches limits despite proper consultation and methodological application, with scholarly consensus (*ijmāʿ*) confirming its application to matters where individuals cannot determine optimal action through rational analysis alone.[297] Sequential integration involves completing systematic *muwāzanāt* analysis, engaging qualified consultation, applying *istikhārah* for divine guidance regarding implementation and timing, then implementing decisions with confidence that both human analytical capacity and divine guidance have been utilized.

If *istishārah* provides breadth of knowledge, *istikhārah* provides depth of orientation. After the exhaustion of rational tools, including two rounds of consultation, the scholarly council turns inward to acknowledge its limits. The Kuwaiti Encyclopedia of Islamic Jurisprudence confirms this consensus

---

[295] Ibn al-Qayyim, *Al-Wābil al-Ṣayyib*, 175.

[296] The Prophetic precedents include military strategy consultations during the Battle of Badr, diplomatic consultations regarding the Treaty of Ḥudaybiyyah, and administrative consultations concerning community governance. The Quranic verse is from al-Shūrā 42:38.

[297] The Kuwaiti Encyclopedia of Islamic Jurisprudence confirms this consensus across the four schools. The theological foundation recognizes that divine knowledge encompasses consequences and implications transcending human analytical capacity, enabling Allah to guide believers toward optimal decisions when systematic *muwāzanāt* analysis yields inconclusive results.

across the four schools. The theological foundation recognizes that divine knowledge encompasses consequences and implications transcending human analytical capacity, enabling Allah to guide believers toward optimal decisions when systematic *muwāzanāt* analysis yields inconclusive results.

The prayer of *istikhārah* encapsulates this recognition: "O Allah, if You know this matter is good for me in my religion, my life, and my ultimate destiny, then decree it for me, make it easy, and bless me in it. But if You know it is bad for me in my religion, my life, and my ultimate destiny, then turn it away from me, turn me away from it, and decree for me what is good wherever it may be, and make me content with it."[298]

This supplication aligns precisely with the aims of *fiqh al-muwāzanāt*. It seeks what is good for religion, worldly affairs, and long-term consequence. In this sense, *istikhārah* is not merely a private devotional act but an integral part of juristic methodology. It acknowledges that after the jurists have fulfilled their duty of reasoning, analysis, and consultation, there remains an unseen dimension of outcomes that only God can know.

For a scholarly council, performing *istikhārah* collectively instills unity of heart. It shifts the frame from intellectual rivalry to shared submission before the Divine. Moreover, it enables scholars to move forward decisively even in the face of lingering uncertainty, confident that they have sought both the wisdom of creation and the guidance of the Creator.

Many scholars hold the view that istikhārah is in matters where the servant does not know where the right course lies. As for that whose goodness is already known, such as acts of worship and righteous deeds, or that whose evil is already known – such as sins and reprehensible acts – there is no need for istikhārah therein, except if one seeks to determine a specific circumstance, such as whether to perform ḥajj in a particular year when there may be danger or discord, or with regard to the company of companions – should he accompany a particular person or not?[299]

Al-Shawkānī (rA) said: "His statement 'in all matters' indicates generality, and that a person should not consider a matter too insignificant due to its

---

[298] Ṣaḥīḥ al-Bukhārī, no. 1162.
[299] *Al-Mawsū'ah al-Fiqhiyyah*, 3:242; Ibn 'Allān, *Al-Fatūḥāt al-Rabbāniyyah*, 1:347.

smallness or lack of importance, such that he leaves off istikhārah therein. For perhaps a matter deemed insignificant may bring great harm in undertaking it or in leaving it. For this reason, the Prophet ﷺ said: 'Let one of you ask his Lord even in the strap of his sandal.'"[300]

Integration within Fiqh al-Muwāzanāt

The integration of *istishārah* and *istikhārah* at this advanced stage of deliberation safeguards the juristic process from three distortions.

- Epistemic narrowness is countered by returning to consultation and widening the circle of expertise.
- Spiritual arrogance is countered by recourse to *istikhārah*, recognizing that no reasoning, however sound, is infallible.
- Practical paralysis is countered by the combination of both, which enables the council to act with humility yet also with conviction.

Thus, the second-level use of *istishārah* and *istikhārah* is not a sign of weakness but of maturity. It demonstrates that juristic leadership acknowledges both the limits of reason and the necessity of trust in God. This methodology does not diminish the rigor of *fiqh al-muwāzanāt* but enriches it, allowing jurists to weigh with both breadth and depth.

6.3. Is Drawing Lots (Qurʿah) a Permissible Final Resort?

Drawing lots represents a specialized mechanism, applied when interests prove genuinely equivalent after comprehensive analysis, consultation, and *istikhārah*, with ʿIzz ibn ʿAbd al-Salām establishing: "When interests are equal, with the impossibility of combining them, then precedence and postponement are left to chance through lot-drawing."[301] Al-Qarāfī clarifies that lot-drawing only applies when competing rights or interests are genuinely equal, providing resolution when analytical methods cannot establish clear precedence, with Quranic precedents including Maryam's guardian selection and Prophet Yūnus, while Prophetic applications include administrative decisions, though this **rare** practice requires unique circumstances and doesn't replace silence or neutrality when they are better options.[302] While classical

[300] Al-Shawkānī, *Nayl al-Awṭār*. 3:315.

[301] This applies particularly to Muslim American communities when multiple equally qualified candidates seek the same leadership position or when determining priority among equivalent community projects with limited resources.

[302] Al-Qarāfī states: "When truth or interest is specifically determined, it is not permissible to deviate from it through lot-drawing, because such deviation abandons known guidance for uncertain alternatives."

jurisprudence recognizes drawing lots (*qur'ah*) for genuinely equivalent choices, its specialized nature and rare application make it less relevant for contemporary American Muslim political contexts.

6.4. Integration and Sequential Application

The alternative mechanisms operate within hierarchical sequence reflecting their relationship to human analytical capacity and divine guidance systems. The methodology begins with comprehensive *muwāzanāt* analysis, progresses to qualified consultation when analysis yields inconclusive results, advances to *istikhārah* when consultation confirms analytical limitations, and concludes with lot-drawing only when all previous approaches demonstrate genuine equivalence between competing alternatives.

For Muslim American political engagement, this sequential approach provides structured decision-making when communities face complex choices about electoral participation, policy advocacy priorities, or coalition strategies. Each mechanism supplements rather than replaces previous analytical work, building upon systematic *muwāzanāt* methodology while preventing misuse as substitutes for rigorous jurisprudential analysis.

Contemporary application requires careful attention to classical limitations while adapting procedural implementation to modern contexts. The sequential integration of consultation and *istikhārah* provides comprehensive resolution capacity when systematic *muwāzanāt* analysis reaches its analytical limits through proper methodological application. The framework's sophistication lies in its recognition that optimal decision-making integrates multiple sources of guidance while maintaining methodological integrity and preventing misuse of alternative mechanisms as substitutes for rigorous jurisprudential analysis and community leadership responsibility.

Conclusion

Fiqh al-muwāzanāt provides American Muslims with a sophisticated framework for navigating complex political landscapes while maintaining fidelity to Islamic principles. Rooted in classical jurisprudential traditions yet responsive to contemporary realities, this approach offers a methodological path between rigid textualism and unmoored pragmatism. The principles of evaluating benefits and harms, prioritizing interests according to their importance, considering consequences, and acknowledging contextual factors

---

Quranic precedents are found in Āl 'Imrān 3:44 and al-Ṣāffāt 37:141, with Prophetic applications including selecting companions for travel.

collectively enable nuanced engagement with political questions facing Muslim communities.

From electoral participation to coalition-building, legislative advocacy to social activism, abortion debates to sexuality and gender-related policies, these principles guide decision-making in ways that honor both religious commitment and practical wisdom. Recent examples include Muslim communities grappling with whether to participate in Democratic primaries to unseat genocide-enablers despite the party's institutional commitment to Israeli apartheid, or evaluating involvement in campus protests knowing they face coordinated suppression through IHRA-based policies and doxxing campaigns funded by pro-Israel organizations.

Nevertheless, significant challenges remain in developing systematic, authoritative, and transparent approaches to applying these principles in the American context. Addressing these challenges requires institutional development, educational initiatives, and interdisciplinary engagement that can strengthen the methodological foundations of fiqh al-muwāzanāt while making it more accessible to community members.

As American Muslim communities continue to navigate their political identity and engagement, *fiqh al-muwāzanāt* offers not only practical guidance for specific questions but also a methodological approach that balances principled commitment with contextual awareness. This balance will remain essential as Muslims seek to contribute to American society while maintaining their distinctive identity and values in an increasingly complex political landscape.

The systematic framework presented in this book represents a significant contribution to English-language Islamic jurisprudence, providing both theoretical foundation and practical methodology for one of the most pressing challenges facing contemporary Muslim communities. Through rigorous application of classical principles to modern contexts, *fiqh al-muwāzanāt* demonstrates the continued relevance and sophistication of Islamic legal reasoning in addressing the complexities of minority Muslim political engagement in pluralistic societies.

7

Conclusion: Toward a Living Jurisprudence

The systematic articulation of fiqh al-muwāzanāt presented in this work represents both culmination and commencement—the crystallization of centuries of Islamic jurisprudential wisdom and the inauguration of methodological frameworks essential for navigating contemporary complexities. As Muslim communities, particularly in minority contexts, confront unprecedented challenges requiring sophisticated balancing of competing interests, benefits, and harms, this methodology transcends academic exercise to become practical necessity.

7.1. Synthesis of Methodological Foundations

The essential conditions—mastery of maqāṣid, verification of effective causes (taḥqīq al-manāṭ), contextual understanding (fiqh al-wāqiʿ), consequential analysis (iʿtibār al-maʾālāt), and priority determination (fiqh al-awlawiyyāt)—constitute an integrated framework rather than discrete requirements. Their synergistic operation enables what great scholars characterized as the distinguishing mark of profound jurisprudential insight: the capacity to place everything in its proper rank justly, whether rulings, values, or actions, then prioritize them correctly based on proper sharʿī standards.

The three typologies of balancing (i.e., between competing benefits, between conflicting harms, and between benefits and harms) provide systematic approaches to scenarios that classical texts addressed through dispersed precedents. This systematization responds to the observation that the sharīʿah came as a balanced whole, not accepting division or separation, requiring contemporary scholars to develop frameworks that honor this holistic vision while addressing novel complexities.

7.2. Contemporary Imperatives and Future Trajectories

The post-2023 global landscape has intensified the urgency of sophisticated muwāzanāt applications in the political realm. The systematic targeting of Palestinian or Muslim advocacy, algorithmic governance of essential services, and transformation of fundamental human interactions through digital mediation exemplify contexts where simplistic jurisprudential responses prove inadequate. Three trajectories emerge as essential for advancing fiqh al-muwāzanāt scholarship:

1. Institutional Sophistication

The transition from individual scholarly opinions to systematic institutional frameworks represents the natural evolution of Islamic legal reasoning in complex societies. Future development requires establishing specialized research centers dedicated to muwāzanāt methodology, creating databases documenting reasoning processes and outcomes for precedential learning, and developing certification programs ensuring methodological competency among practitioners. The Assembly of Muslim Jurists of America's recent initiatives toward collective deliberation protocols provide nascent models requiring expansion and refinement.

2. Interdisciplinary Integration

The artificial intelligence revolution exemplifies domains where traditional jurisprudential rulings alone proves insufficient. Future muwāzanāt applications demand structured collaboration between Islamic legal scholars and domain specialists—computer scientists for AI governance, psychologists for digital platform impacts, political scientists for civic engagement strategies. This integration must transcend superficial consultation to achieve what may envisioned as fiqh "teams" (firaq fiqhiyyah) combining diverse expertise within unified methodological frameworks.

With AI in particular, the Sharīʿah's approach to human action is neither technologically naïve nor reactionary. It begins from the accountability of the mukallaf, the protection of rights, the preservation of truth, the fulfillment of trusts, the avoidance of harm, and the pursuit of benefit within divine limits. AI has no taqwa, no *dhimmah*, no *niyyah*, no wilayah, and no accountability before Allah. The machine is not the moral subject. Yet the human beings who design, deploy, market, use, rely upon, conceal, share, and profit from AI remain accountable for their actions and omissions. This distinction is foundational. It prevents the anthropomorphizing of AI while also preventing humans from hiding behind the machine.

The jurist must first conceptualize the case accurately, verify the effective legal description, understand the technological reality, identify the baseline ruling, distinguish *taklīfī* from *waḍʿī* consequences, weigh benefits and harms, consider likely outcomes, and then apply the ruling with its conditions and limits. This method is not a concession to modern complexity. It is part of the inherited discipline of *iftāʾ*. The tradition's resources—*taḥqīq al-manāṭ, fiqh al-wāqiʿ, maqāṣid, qawāʿid, sadd al-dharāʾiʿ, iʿtibār al-maʾālāt, fiqh al-awlawiyyāt, amanah, daman,* and *tabayyun*—are not relics of a pre-digital age. They are precisely the tools needed when moral agency is shaped by systems whose harms may be personalized, hidden, scalable, and cumulative.

3. Pedagogical Development

The incorporation of fiqh al-muwāzanāt into formal Islamic legal curricula remains uncommon despite its practical necessity. Future scholarship must develop comprehensive pedagogical materials including case study repositories demonstrating successful applications, simulation exercises training students in balancing methodologies, and assessment tools measuring competency in reasoning. The transition from theoretical understanding to practical application requires educational innovations matching the sophistication of contemporary challenges.

7.3. Preserving Authenticity Within Adaptation

The systematization of muwāzanāt methodology raises legitimate concerns about preserving Islamic legal tradition's spiritual and communal dimensions. The danger in our age is not the absence of ijtihād, but rather ijtihād by those unqualified, who possess neither the tools nor the spirit (rūḥ) of true jurisprudential insight. The framework presented herein addresses these concerns through multiple safeguards: required scholarly prerequisites preventing unqualified practice, collective deliberation requirements tempering individual perspectives, and emphasis on maqāṣid ensuring connection to divine purposes rather than utilitarian calculation.

The relationship between systematic methodology and spiritual insight (*baṣīrah*) merits particular emphasis. While this work has focused on analytical frameworks, the Islamic tradition consistently affirms that profound jurisprudential wisdom emerges from synthesizing rigorous reasoning with spiritual refinement. Ultimately, religious knowledge (*ʿilm*) is light that Allah casts into the heart of whomever He wills, which means that methodological sophistication must complement rather than replace traditional emphases on spiritual development.

7.4. A Living Jurisprudence for Dynamic Challenges

The title of this conclusion, "Toward a Living Jurisprudence," captures the essential vision animating fiqh al-muwāzanāt. Islamic law's vitality depends upon its capacity to address contemporary realities while maintaining fidelity to revelatory foundations. This dynamic interaction between permanence and change, between universal principles and contextual applications, finds systematic expression through muwāzanāt methodology.

The challenges confronting Muslim communities, from navigating hostile political environments to governing emerging technologies, will only intensify in complexity. Traditional approaches alternating between rigid literalism and unprincipled accommodation prove equally inadequate. Fiqh al-muwāzanāt offers a third path: principled flexibility grounded in systematic methodology, enabling communities to pursue authentic Islamic flourishing within contemporary contexts.

Final Reflections

This work commenced with recognition that Muslim communities face unprecedented challenges requiring sophisticated jurisprudential approaches. The systematic framework presented provides structured methodology for addressing these complexities. Yet methodology alone remains insufficient without committed scholars willing to undertake the demanding work of contemporary ijtihād, communities prepared to support and implement scholarly guidance, and institutions capable of sustaining collective deliberation across time and space.

The Prophet ﷺ declared, "Allah will raise for this community at the beginning of every century those who will renew its religion."[303] In our era of accelerating change and multiplying challenges, this renewal (*tajdīd*) requires not merely individual reformers but systematic methodologies enabling continuous adaptation while preserving Islamic principles. Fiqh al-muwāzanāt

[303] Sunan Abī Dāwūd, no. 4291.

represents one essential component of this broader renewal, providing frameworks through which the eternal guidance of revelation engages the temporal complexities of human experience.

As this work concludes, it issues a polite call to three constituencies: to scholars, that they master and refine these methodologies while maintaining spiritual grounding; to institutions, that they develop infrastructure supporting sophisticated collective reasoning; and to communities, that they recognize the complexity of contemporary challenges while trusting in the Islamic tradition's capacity to provide authentic guidance. The path forward requires neither naive optimism nor paralyzing despair, but rather the confident application of systematic methodology grounded in divine guidance and scholarly wisdom.

May Allah guide our efforts toward that which pleases Him
and benefits His creation.

وَآخِرُ دَعْوَانَا أَنِ الْحَمْدُ لِلَّهِ رَبِّ الْعَالَمِينَ

Glossary

ʿādah (عادة) - *pl. ʿādāt* - Custom, habit, or cultural practice that may have legal implications

adillah (أدلة) - *sing. dalīl* - Legal evidences or proofs

afḍal (أفضل) - Superior, more excellent, preferable

ahl al-khibrah (أهل الخبرة) - People of expertise in a particular field

aḥkām (أحكام) - *sing. ḥukm* - Legal rulings, judgments

ʿaql (عقل) - Intellect, reason; one of the five necessities (ḍarūriyyāt)

aṣl (أصل) - *pl. uṣūl* - Foundation, origin, principle

awlawiyyāt (أولويات) - Priorities

ḍarar (ضرر) - Harm, damage, injury

ḍarūrah (ضرورة) - *pl. ḍarūrāt* - Necessity, dire need

ḍarūriyyāt (ضروريات) - The essential necessities; the fundamental interests protected by Islamic law

dharīʿah (ذريعة) - *pl. dharāʾiʿ* - Means; that which leads to something else

dhāt (ذات) - Essence, intrinsic nature

dīn (دين) - Religion; one of the five necessities

faqīh (فقيه) - *pl. fuqahāʾ* - Jurist, scholar of Islamic law

farḍ ʿayn (فرض عين) - Individual obligation

farḍ kifāyah (فرض كفاية) - Communal obligation

farʿ (فرع) - *pl. furūʿ* - Branch, derivative, secondary matter

fatwā (فتوى) - *pl. fatāwā* - Legal opinion, religious edict

fiqh (فقه) - Islamic jurisprudence, understanding

fiqh al-awlawiyyāt (فقه الأولويات) - Jurisprudence of priorities

fiqh al-muwāzanāt (فقه الموازنات) - Jurisprudence of balancing interests

fiqh al-wāqiʿ (فقه الواقع) - Jurisprudence of reality/context

fitnah (فتنة) - Trial, discord, civil strife

ghāyah (غاية) - *pl. ghāyāt* - Goal, objective, end purpose

ḥājah (حاجة) - *pl. ḥājiyyāt* - Need; the second level of maqāṣid

ḥalāl (حلال) - Permissible, lawful

ḥaraj (حرج) - Hardship, difficulty, constriction

ḥarām (حرام) - Forbidden, prohibited

ḥikmah (حكمة) - Wisdom; the underlying wisdom behind a ruling

ḥukm (حكم) - *pl. aḥkām* - Ruling, judgment, legal decision

iʿtibār al-maʾālāt (اعتبار المآلات) - Consideration of consequences

ijmāʿ (إجماع) - Consensus; one of the sources of Islamic law

ijtihād (اجتهاد) - Independent legal reasoning, scholarly effort
ijtihād jamāʿī (اجتهاد جماعي) - Collective ijtihād
ʿillah (علة) - *pl. ʿilal* - Effective cause, ratio legis
istiḥsān (استحسان) - Juristic preference; departure from strict analogy
istishārah (استشارة) - Consultation, seeking counsel
istikhārah (استخارة) - Seeking divine guidance through prayer
istiṣlāḥ (استصلاح) - Consideration of public interest
khāṣṣ (خاص) - Specific, particular, private
khayr (خير) - Good, benefit, welfare
maʾāl (مآل) - *pl. maʾālāt* - Consequence, outcome, eventual result
madhhab (مذهب) - *pl. madhāhib* - School of Islamic jurisprudence
mafsadah (مفسدة) - *pl. mafāsid* - Harm, evil, corruption
manāṭ (مناط) - Locus, basis, or operative cause of a ruling
mandūb (مندوب) - Recommended, encouraged but not obligatory
maqāṣid (مقاصد) - *sing. maqṣad* - Objectives, goals of Islamic law
maqāṣid al-sharīʿah (مقاصد الشريعة) - The objectives of Islamic law
maṣlaḥah (مصلحة) - *pl. maṣāliḥ* - Benefit, interest, welfare
maṣlaḥah mursalah (مصلحة مرسلة) - Unrestricted/unattested public interest
maytah (ميتة) - Carrion, dead meat
muḥallil (محلل) - Mediator in a race or competition
mujtahid (مجتهد) - One qualified to perform ijtihād
mukallaf (مكلف) - Legally responsible person
munkar (منكر) - Evil, wrong, that which is rejected
muqaddam (مقدم) - Given precedence, prioritized
muwāzanah (موازنة) - Balancing, weighing, comparison
nafs (نفس) - Soul, life; one of the five necessities
naql (نقل) - Transmitted knowledge, revelation
nasl (نسل) - Progeny, lineage; one of the five necessities
naṣṣ (نص) - *pl. nuṣūṣ* - Text, explicit textual evidence
nawʿ (نوع) - *pl. anwāʿ* - Type, kind, category
nawāzil (نوازل) - *sing. nāzilah* - New cases, unprecedented issues
qāʿidah (قاعدة) - *pl. qawāʿid* - Principle, maxim, rule
qaṭʿī (قطعي) - Definitive, certain, conclusive
qiyās (قياس) - Analogical reasoning; one of the sources of Islamic law
sadd al-dharāʾiʿ (سد الذرائع) - Blocking the means (to evil)
sharīʿah (شريعة) - Islamic law, the divine path
shubhah (شبهة) - *pl. shubuhāt* - Doubt, ambiguity, resemblance

shūrā (شورى) - Consultation, mutual deliberation
ta'āruḍ (تعارض) - Conflict, contradiction, opposition
taḥqīq al-manāṭ (تحقيق المناط) - Verification of the effective cause
taḥsīn (تحسين) - *pl. taḥsīniyyāt* - Improvement, embellishment; the third level of maqāṣid
takhrīj al-manāṭ (تخريج المناط) - Extraction of the effective cause
taklīf (تكليف) - Legal responsibility, religious obligation
tanqīḥ al-manāṭ (تنقيح المناط) - Refinement of the effective cause
tanzīl (تنزيل) - Application, implementation of rulings to reality
tarjīḥ (ترجيح) - Preponderance, giving preference, prioritization
tawḥīd (توحيد) - Monotheism, divine unity
'ulamā' (علماء) - *sing. 'ālim* - Scholars, learned ones
ummah (أمة) - The Muslim community
'urf (عرف) - Custom, common practice
uṣūl al-fiqh (أصول الفقه) - Principles of Islamic jurisprudence
wājib (واجب) - Obligatory, required
wāqi' (واقع) - Reality, actual circumstances, context
wasīlah (وسيلة) - *pl. wasā'il* - Means, method, instrument
ẓann (ظن) - Probability, presumption, speculative knowledge
ẓannī (ظني) - Speculative, probable, non-definitive

Bibliography

'Alwānī, Ṭāhā Jābir al-. *Uṣūl al-Fiqh al-Islāmī: Manāhij al-Baḥth wa-l-Ma'rifah.* Herndon: International Institute of Islamic Thought, 1995.

Abū Dāwūd, Sulaymān ibn al-Ash'ath. *Sunan Abī Dāwūd.* Riyadh: Dār al-Salām, 1999.

Abū Zahrah, Muḥammad. *Abū Ḥanīfah.* Cairo: Dār al-Fikr al-'Arabī, n.d.

Abū Zahrah, Muḥammad. *Uṣūl al-Fiqh* [Principles of Jurisprudence]. Cairo: Dār al-Fikr al-'Arabī, 1958.

al-Āmidī, Sayf al-Dīn 'Alī b. Muḥammad. *Al-Iḥkām fī Uṣūl al-Aḥkām* [The Definitive in the Principles of Rulings]. 4 vols. Beirut: Dār al-Kutub al-'Ilmiyyah, 1983.

al-Bukhārī, Muḥammad ibn Ismā'īl. *Ṣaḥīḥ al-Bukhārī.* Riyadh: Dār al-Salām, 1999.

al-Būṭī, Muḥammad Sa'īd Ramaḍān. *Ḍawābiṭ al-Maṣlaḥah* [Controls of Public Interest]. Damascus: Dār al-Fikr, n.d.

al-Dirīnī, Muḥammad Fathī. *Buḥūth Muqāranah fī al-Fiqh al-Islāmī wa-Uṣūlih.* 1st ed. Beirut: Mu'assasat al-Risālah, 1994.

al-Dūrī, 'Abd al-'Azīz. *Al-Nuẓum al-Islāmiyyah* [Islamic Systems]. Beirut: Markaz Dirāsāt al-Waḥdah al-'Arabiyyah, 1993.

al-Ghazālī, Abū Ḥāmid. *Al-Mustaṣfā min 'Ilm al-Uṣūl.* Edited by Muḥammad 'Abd al-Salām 'Abd al-Shāfī. 2 vols. Beirut: Dār al-Kutub al-'Ilmiyyah, 1993.

al-Ghazālī, Abū Ḥāmid. *Iḥyā' 'Ulūm al-Dīn* [Reviving the Religious Sciences]. Beirut: Dār al-Ma'rifah, n.d.

al-Ghazālī, Muḥammad. *Fiqh al-Sīrah.* Damascus: Dār al-Qalam, 1991.

al-Ghazālī, Muḥammad. *Kayfa Nata'āmal ma'a al-Qur'ān.* Damascus: Dār al-Shāmiyyah, 1999.

al-Ḥusayn, Walīd b. 'Alī. *I'tibār Ma'ālāt al-Af'āl wa-Atharuhā al-Fiqhī.* 2 vols. Riyāḍ: Dār al-Tadmuriyyah, 2009.

Ali, Kecia. "Muslims and Meat-Eating." *Journal of Religious Ethics* 43, no. 2 (2015): 268-288.

al-Kamālī, 'Abd Allāh Yaḥyā. *Ta'ṣīl fiqh al-muwāzanāt.* Beirut: Dār Ibn Ḥazm, 2000.

al-Mawsū'ah al-Kuwaytiyyah [Kuwaiti Encyclopedia]. 45 vols. Kuwait: Wizārat al-Awqāf wa-al-Shu'ūn al-Islāmiyyah, 1983–2006.

al-Mīmān, Nāṣir. *Al-Qawā'id wa-al-ḍawābiṭ al-fiqhiyya 'inda Shaykh al-Islām Ibn Taymiyya fī Kitābay "al-Ṭahārah wa-al-Ṣalāh".* Master's thesis, Umm al-Qurā University, 1993.

al-Nadwī, 'Ali Aḥmad. *Al-Qawā'id al-fiqhiyya.* Damascus: Dār al-Qalam, 1987.

al-Najjār, 'Abd al-Majīd 'Umar. *Fuṣūl fī al-Fikr al-Islāmī bi-l-Maghrib.* 1st ed. Beirut: Dār al-Gharb al-Islāmī, 1412/1992.

al-Najjār, 'Abd al-Majīd. *Khilāfat al-Insān bayna al-Waḥy wa-al-'Aql.* Beirut: Dār al-Gharb al-Islāmī, 1987.

al-Najjār, 'Abd al-Majīd. *Maqāṣid al-Sharī'ah bi-Ab'ād Jadīdah*. 2nd ed. Beirut: Dār al-Gharb al-Islāmī, 2008.

al-Nawawī, Yaḥyā ibn Sharaf. *Al-Majmū' Sharḥ al-Muhadhdhab*. 20 vols. Beirut: Dār al-Fikr, 1996.

al-Nawawī, Yaḥyā ibn Sharaf. *Rawḍat al-Ṭālibīn wa-'Umdat al-Muftīn*. Edited by Zuhayr al-Shāwīsh. Beirut: al-Maktab al-Islāmī, 1991.

al-Qaraḍāwī, Yūsuf. *Al-Ṣaḥwah al-Islāmiyyah bayna al-Juhūd wa al-Taṭarruf*. Cairo: Dār al-Shurūq, 2001.

al-Qaraḍāwī, Yūsuf. *Al-Siyāsah al-Shar'iyyah*. Cairo: Dār al-Shurūq, 2006.

al-Qaraḍāwī, Yūsuf. *Dirāsah fī Fiqh Maqāṣid al-Sharī'ah*. Cairo: Dār al-Shurūq, 2006.

al-Qaraḍāwī, Yūsuf. *Fī Fiqh al-Awlawiyyāt: Dirāsah Jadīdah fī Ḍaw' al-Qur'ān wa al-Sunnah* [Jurisprudence of Priorities]. Cairo: Maktabat Wahbah, 1996.

al-Qaraḍāwī, Yūsuf. *Fiqh al-Wāqi': Dirāsāt fī Ishkāliyyāt al-Ḥarakah al-Islāmiyyah al-Mu'āṣirah*. Cairo: Maktabat Wahbah, 2007.

al-Qaraḍāwī, Yūsuf. *Madkhal li-Dirāsat al-Sharī'ah al-Islāmiyyah*. Cairo: Maktabat Wahbah, 2001.

al-Qarāfī, Shihāb al-Dīn Aḥmad b. Idrīs. *Al-Furūq*. 4 vols. Beirut: Dār al-Kutub al-'Ilmiyyah, 1998.

al-Qarāfī, Shihāb al-Dīn. *Al-Iḥkām fī Tamyīz al-Fatāwā 'an al-Aḥkām wa-Taṣarrufāt al-Qāḍī wa-l-Imām*. Edited by 'Abd al-Fattāḥ Abū Ghuddah. 2nd ed. Beirut: Dār al-Bashā'ir al-Islāmiyyah, 1995.

al-Qarāfī, Shihāb al-Dīn. *Sharḥ Tanqīḥ al-Fuṣūl*. Cairo: Sharikat al-Ṭibā'ah al-Fanniyyah al-Muttaḥidah, 1973.

al-Qurṭubī, Muḥammad ibn Aḥmad. *Al-Jāmi' li-Aḥkām al-Qur'ān*. 20 vols. Beirut: Dār al-Kutub al-'Ilmiyyah, 1996.

al-Rabwa'ah, Aḥmad Ḥasan. "Al-Muwāzanah bayna al-maṣāliḥ wa-al-mafāsid wa-taṭbīqātuhumā fī al-wāqi' al-mu'āṣir" [The Balancing of Interests and Harms and Their Applications in Contemporary Reality]. *Journal of Scientific Research and Islamic Studies* 12, no. 1 (2020): 65–90.

al-Raysūnī, Aḥmad. *Naẓariyyat al-Maqāṣid 'inda al-Imām al-Shāṭibī*. Herndon: International Institute of Islamic Thought, 1995.

al-Rāzī, Fakhr al-Dīn. *Al-Maḥṣūl fī 'Ilm Uṣūl al-Fiqh*. Beirut: Mu'assasat al-Risālah, 1997.

al-Sa'dī, 'Abd al-Ḥakīm 'Abd al-Raḥmān. *Mabāḥith al-'Illah fī al-Qiyās 'inda al-Uṣūliyyīn* [Discussions on Causality in Analogy among Methodologists]. 1st ed. Beirut: Dār al-Bashā'ir al-Islāmiyyah, 2000.

al-Sanūsī, 'Abd al-Raḥmān b. Ma'mar. *I'tibār al-Ma'ālāt wa-Murā'āt Nata'ij al-Taṣarrufāt: Dirāsah Muqāranah fī Uṣūl al-Fiqh wa-Maqāṣid al-Sharī'ah*. Dammām: Dār Ibn al-Jawzī, 1424 AH / 2003 CE.

al-Shāfi'ī, Muḥammad ibn Idrīs. *Al-Risālah*. Edited by Aḥmad Muḥammad Shākir. Cairo: Dār al-Turāth, 1979.

al-Shāṭibī, Abū Isḥāq. *Al-I'tiṣām*. Beirut: Dār Ibn 'Affān, 1997.

al-Shāṭibī, Abū Isḥāq. *Al-Muwāfaqāt fī Uṣūl al-Sharī'ah*. Edited by 'Abd Allah Darrāz. 4 vols. Beirut: Dār al-Kutub al-'Ilmiyyah, 2003.

al-Shawkānī, Muḥammad ibn 'Alī. *Irshād al-Fuḥūl ilā Taḥqīq al-Ḥaqq min 'Ilm al-Uṣūl*. Edited by Muḥammad Ṣubḥī ibn Ḥasan Ḥallāq. 2 vols. Damascus: Dār Ibn Kathīr, 1443 AH.

al-Shinqīṭī, Aḥmad 'Abd al-Wahhāb. *Al-Waṣf al-Munāsib li-Shar' al-Ḥukm*. Medina: Markaz al-Baḥth al-'Ilmī wa-Iḥyā' al-'Ilm al-Islāmī, 1994.

al-Suyūṭī, Jalāl al-Dīn. *Al-Ashbāh wa-al-Naẓā'ir*. Beirut: Dār al-Kutub al-'Ilmiyyah, 1983.

al-Ṭabarī, Muḥammad ibn Jarīr. *Jāmi' al-Bayān fī Ta'wīl al-Qur'ān*. Edited by Aḥmad Muḥammad Shākir. 15 vols. Beirut: Mu'assasat al-Risālah, 2000.

al-Tinbuktī, Muḥammad b. Aḥmad. *Al-Qawā'id al-Uṣūlīyyah 'inda Ibn Taymiyyah*. 2 vols. Beirut: Dār Ibn Ḥazm, 1429/2008.

al-Tirmidhī, Muḥammad ibn 'Īsā. *Sunan al-Tirmidhī*. Riyadh: Dār al-Salām, 1999.

al-Turkī, Ḥasan, ed. *Uṣūl al-Fiqh al-Islāmī*. 2 vols. Riyadh: Dār al-Waṭan, 1996.

al-Zankī, Najm al-Dīn Qādir Karīm. *Al-Ijtihād fī Mawridi al-Naṣṣ: Dirāsah Uṣūlīyyah Muqāranah*. 1st ed. Beirut: Dār al-Kutub al-'Ilmiyyah, 1427/2006.

al-Zarqā', Muṣṭafā. *Al-Madkhal al-fiqhī al-'āmm*. Damascus: Dār al-Qalam, 2004.

al-Zuḥaylī, Wahbah. *Al-Fiqh al-Islāmī wa-Adillatuh* [Islamic Jurisprudence and Its Evidences]. 8 vols. Damascus: Dār al-Fikr, 1997.

al-Zuḥaylī, Wahbah. *Uṣūl al-Fiqh*. 2 vols. Damascus: Dār al-Fikr, 1986.

Angwin, Julia, Jeff Larson, Surya Mattu, and Lauren Kirchner. "Machine Bias." *ProPublica*, May 23, 2016.

Arthur, W. Brian. "Competing Technologies, Increasing Returns, and Lock-In by Historical Events." *The Economic Journal* 99, no. 394 (1989): 116-131.

Auda, Jasser. *Maqasid al-Shariah as Philosophy of Islamic Law: A Systems Approach*. London: International Institute of Islamic Thought, 2008.

Ayub, Muhammad. *Understanding Islamic Finance*. Chichester: John Wiley & Sons, 2007.

Barocas, Solon, and Andrew D. Selbst. "Big Data's Disparate Impact." *California Law Review* 104 (2016): 671-732.

Bartlett, Robert, Adair Morse, Richard Stanton, and Nancy Wallace. "Consumer-Lending Discrimination in the FinTech Era." *Journal of Financial Economics* 143, no. 1 (2022): 30-56.

Bdeir, Rā'id 'Abd Allāh. *Al-Manāṭ fī Uṣūl al-Fiqh*. 1st ed. Cairo: Dār Ibn al-Jawzī, 1427/2006.

Boyd, Danah. *It's Complicated: The Social Lives of Networked Teens*. New Haven: Yale University Press, 2014.

Bunt, Gary R. *Hashtag Islam: How Cyber-Islamic Environments Are Transforming Religious Authority*. Chapel Hill: University of North Carolina Press, 2018.

Council on American-Islamic Relations (CAIR). *2024 Voter Guide: Principles Over Parties*. Washington, DC: CAIR, 2024.

Crawford, Kate. *Atlas of AI: Power, Politics, and the Planetary Costs of Artificial Intelligence*. New Haven: Yale University Press, 2021.

Dignum, Virginia. *Responsible Artificial Intelligence: How to Develop and Use AI in a Responsible Way*. Cham: Springer, 2019.

ECFR (European Council for Fatwa and Research). *Islamic Legal Verdicts*. n.p.: n.d.

El-Gamal, Mahmoud. *Islamic Finance*. New York: Palgrave Macmillan, 2006.

Eubanks, Virginia. *Automating Inequality: How High-Tech Tools Profile, Police, and Punish the Poor*. New York: St. Martin's Press, 2018.

Ferguson, Andrew Guthrie. *The Rise of Big Data Policing: Surveillance, Race, and the Future of Law Enforcement*. New York: NYU Press, 2017.

Gāwush, Aḥmad. *Al-Ijtihād 'inda al-Uṣūliyyīn: Min al-Naẓariyyah ilā al-Taṭbīq* [Ijtihad among Methodologists: From Theory to Application]. 1st ed. Beirut: Dār Ibn Ḥazm, 2009.

Gillespie, Tarleton. *Custodians of the Internet: Platforms, Content Moderation, and the Hidden Decisions That Shape Social Media*. New Haven: Yale University Press, 2018.

Ḥajar al-Haytamī, Ibn. *Tuḥfat al-Muḥtāj fī Sharḥ al-Minhāj* [The Gift of the Needy in Commenting on the Curriculum]. 10 vols. Cairo: al-Maktabah al-Tijāriyyah al-Kubrā, 1983.

Ḥajar, Ibn. *Fatḥ al-Bārī*. 13 vols. Beirut: Dār al-Ma'rifah, 1379 AH.

Hallaq, Wael B. *A History of Islamic Legal Theories: An Introduction to Sunni Usul al-Fiqh*. Cambridge: Cambridge University Press, 1997.

Ḥamīdullāh, Muḥammad. *Majmū'at al-Wathā'iq al-Siyāsiyyah*. Beirut: Dār al-Nafā'is, 1987.

Hishām, Ibn. *Al-Sīrah al-Nabawiyyah*. Edited by al-Saqqā, al-Abyārī, and Shalabī. 4 vols. Cairo, 1955.

Howe, Nicolas. "Secular Iconoclasm: Purifying, Privatizing, and Profaning Public Faith." *Social & Cultural Geography* 10, no. 8 (2009): 849-868.

Ibn 'Abd al-Salām, 'Izz al-Dīn. *Qawā'id al-Aḥkām fī Maṣāliḥ al-Anām*. Beirut: Dār al-Kutub al-'Ilmiyyah, 1999.

Ibn 'Ābidīn. *Radd al-Muḥtār*. Beirut: Dār al-Fikr, 1992.

Ibn al-Najjār al-Ḥanbalī, Muḥammad b. Aḥmad. *Sharḥ al-Kawkab al-Munīr*. Edited by al-Zuḥaylī and Ḥammād. Riyadh: Maktabat 'Ubaykān, 1418/1997.

Ibn al-Qayyim al-Jawziyyah. *I'lām al-Muwaqqi'īn 'an Rabb al-'Ālamīn*. Edited by Muḥammad Ibrāhīm. 4 vols. Beirut: Dār al-Kutub al-'Ilmiyyah, 1991.

Ibn Āshūr, Muḥammad al-Ṭāhir. *Maqāṣid al-Sharī'ah al-Islāmiyyah*. Edited by El-tahir el-Mesnawi. Kuala Lumpur: Al-fajr, 1999.

Ibn Khaldun. *The Muqaddimah: An Introduction to History*. Translated by Franz Rosenthal. 3 vols. Princeton: Princeton University Press, 1967.

Ibn Nujaym. *Al-Ashbāh wa-al-Naẓā'ir*. Beirut: Dār al-Kutub al-'Ilmiyyah, 1999.

Ibn Qudāmah, Muwaffaq al-Dīn. *Rawḍat al-Nāẓir wa-Jannat al-Manāẓir fī Uṣūl al-Fiqh*. 2nd ed. Beirut: Mu'assasat al-Risālah, 1423/2002.

Ibn Taymiyyah. *Al-Radd 'alā al-Manṭiqiyyīn*. Edited by Muḥammad Ḥasan Ismā'īl. 1st ed. Beirut: Dār al-Kutub al-'Ilmiyyah, 1428/2007.

Ibn Taymiyyah. *Al-Siyāsah al-Shar'iyyah*. Riyadh: Wizārat al-Shu'ūn al-Islāmiyyah, 1998.

Ibn Taymiyyah. *Bayān al-Dalīl*. Beirut: Al-Maktab al-Islāmī, 1998.

Ibn Taymiyyah. *Dar' Ta'āruḍ al-'Aql wa-al-Naql*. Edited by Muḥammad Rashād Sālim. 11 vols. Riyadh: Jāmi'at al-Imām Muḥammad b. Sa'ūd al-Islāmiyyah, 1411/1991.

Ibn Taymiyyah. *Majmū' al-Fatāwā* [Collected Fatwas]. Edited by 'Abd al-Raḥmān ibn Qāsim. 37 vols. al-Manṣūrah: Dār al-Wafā', 2005.

Ibn Taymiyyah. *Minhāj al-Sunnah al-Nabawiyyah*. Edited by Muḥammad Rashād Sālim. 8 vols. Riyadh: Jāmi'at al-Imām Muḥammad b. Sa'ūd al-Islāmiyyah, 1406/1986.

Ibn Taymiyyah. *Qā'idah fī al-Maḥabbah*. In *Majmū' al-Fatāwā*, vol. 10. Medina: Majma' al-Malik Fahd, 1995.

IFA (Islamic Fiqh Academy). *Majallat Majma' al-Fiqh al-Islāmī* [Journal of the Islamic Fiqh Academy]. Jeddah: IFA, n.d.

Illouz, Eva. *Cold Intimacies: The Making of Emotional Capitalism*. Cambridge: Polity Press, 2007.

IOMS (Islamic Organization for Medical Sciences). *Contemporary Bioethical Issues*. Kuwait: IOMS, n.d.

IOMS. *Islamic Ethics in Medical Practice*. Kuwait: IOMS, n.d.

Jackson, Sherman A. *Islam and the Blackamerican: Looking Toward the Third Resurrection*. New York: Oxford University Press, 2005.

Jackson, Sherman A. *Islamic Law and the State: The Constitutional Jurisprudence of Shihāb al-Dīn al-Qarāfī*. Leiden: Brill, 2002.

Jadīyah, 'Umar. *Aṣl I'tibār al-Ma'āl bayna al-Naẓariyyah wa-al-Taṭbīq*. Beirut: Dār Ibn Ḥazm, 2009.

Jobin, Anna, Marcello Ienca, and Effy Vayena. "The Global Landscape of AI Ethics Guidelines." *Nature Machine Intelligence* 1, no. 9 (2019): 389-399.

Kamali, Mohammad Hashim. *Maqasid al-Shariah Made Simple*. London: International Institute of Islamic Thought, 2008.

Kamali, Mohammad Hashim. *Principles of Islamic Jurisprudence*. 3rd ed. Cambridge: Islamic Texts Society, 2003.

Khallāf, 'Abd al-Wahhāb. *'Ilm Uṣūl al-Fiqh*. Cairo: Maktabat al-Da'wah al-Islāmiyyah, 1990.

Khan, M. A. Muqtedar. "Artificial Intelligence, Autonomous Weapons and Islamic Ethics." *Journal of Islamic and Muslim Studies* 4, no. 1 (2019): 84-102.

Kitāb al-'Ayn al-Muhmalah. 8 vols. Beirut: Dār al-Kutub al-'Ilmiyyah, n.d.

Koca, Ozgur. "Artificial Intelligence and Islamic Ethics: Selected Preliminary Observations." *Journal of Islamic Ethics* 5, no. 1-2 (2021): 1-30.

Lutz, Christoph, and Gemma Newlands. "Privacy and Smart Speakers: A Multi-Dimensional Approach." *The Information Society* 37, no. 3 (2021): 147-162.

Masud, Muhammad Khalid. "The Doctrine of Siyāsa in Islamic Law." *Recht van de Islam* 18 (2001): 1-29.

Maurer, Bill. *Pious Property: Islamic Mortgages in the United States*. New York: Russell Sage Foundation, 2006.

Mearsheimer, John J., and Stephen M. Walt. *The Israel Lobby and U.S. Foreign Policy*. Updated edition. New York: Farrar, Straus and Giroux, 2006.

Mir-Hosseini, Ziba, and Richard Tapper. "Marriage, Family, and State: Changes in Shari'a-Based Family Law." In *The Oxford Handbook of Contemporary Islam*, edited by John L. Esposito and Emad El-Din Shahin. Oxford: Oxford University Press, 2014.

Moors, Annelies. "Unregistered Islamic Marriages: Anxieties about Sexuality and Islam in the Netherlands." In *The Anthropology of Islam Reader*, edited by Jens Kreinath, 188-200. London: Routledge, 2012.

Muslim, Abū al-Ḥusayn. *Ṣaḥīḥ Muslim*. Riyadh: Dār al-Salām, 1998.

Nissenbaum, Helen. *Privacy in Context: Technology, Policy, and the Integrity of Social Life*. Stanford: Stanford Law School Press, 2010.

Noble, Safiya Umoja. *Algorithms of Oppression: How Search Engines Reinforce Racism*. New York: NYU Press, 2018.

O'Neil, Cathy. *Weapons of Math Destruction: How Big Data Increases Inequality and Threatens Democracy*. New York: Crown, 2016.

Opwis, Felicitas. *Maṣlaḥa and the Purpose of the Law: Islamic Discourse on Legal Change from the 4th/10th to 8th/14th Century*. Leiden: Brill, 2010.

Palestine Legal and Center for Constitutional Rights. *The Palestine Exception to Free Speech*. 2024 Update. New York: Palestine Legal & Center for Constitutional Rights, 2024.

Parker, Geoffrey G., Marshall W. Van Alstyne, and Sangeet Paul Choudary. *Platform Revolution*. New York: W. W. Norton, 2016.

Pew Research Center. "Muslims in America: Immigrants and Those Born in U.S. See Life Differently in Many Ways." August 28, 2018.

Rahwan, Iyad. "Society-in-the-Loop: Programming the Algorithmic Social Contract." *Ethics and Information Technology* 20, no. 1 (2018): 5-14.

Roald, Anne Sofie. *New Muslims in the European Context: The Experience of Scandinavian Converts*. Leiden: Brill, 2004.

Rosenfeld, Michael J., and Reuben J. Thomas. "Searching for a Mate: The Rise of the Internet as a Social Intermediary." *American Sociological Review* 77, no. 4 (2012): 523-547.

Russell, Stuart. *Human Compatible: Artificial Intelligence and the Problem of Control*. New York: Viking, 2019.

Sachedina, Abdulaziz. *Islam and the Challenge of Human Rights*. Oxford: Oxford University Press, 2009.

Scholz, Trebor. *Platform Cooperativism: Challenging the Corporate Sharing Economy*. New York: Rosa Luxemburg Stiftung, 2016.

Schwartz, Barry. *The Paradox of Choice: Why More Is Less*. New York: HarperCollins, 2004.

Shukrī, Farīd. *Fiqh al-Tanzīl*. Rabat: Maṭba'at al-Najāḥ al-Jadīdah, 2015.

Silsilat Kitāb al-Ummah. Fiqh al-Wāqi' Uṣūl wa-Ḍawābiṭ [The Jurisprudence of Reality: Principles and Guidelines]. Issue No. 75. Ministry of Awqāf and Islamic Affairs, Qatar, 2000.

Soroush, Abdolkarim. *Reason, Freedom, and Democracy in Islam*. New York: Oxford University Press, 2000.

Sunstein, Cass R. *#Republic: Divided Democracy in the Age of Social Media*. Princeton: Princeton University Press, 2017.

Topol, Eric. *Deep Medicine: How Artificial Intelligence Can Make Healthcare Human Again*. New York: Basic Books, 2019.

Usmani, Muḥammad Taqī 'Uthmānī. *Introduction to Islamic Finance*. Karachi: Maktabah Ma'ārif al-Qur'ān, n.d.

Zuboff, Shoshana. *The Age of Surveillance Capitalism*. New York: PublicAffairs, 2019.

Index

Appendix A
High-Level Overview:
The Muwāzanāt Decision Matrix

A systematic six-phase process enabling Islamic scholarly councils to make principled decisions when competing interests, benefits, and harms must be carefully balanced according to Islamic legal principles. What follows is a proposed system that can be modified and adopted to varying councils and their respective needs.

Six-Phase Process

Phase 1: Issue Assessment

Objective: Comprehensive understanding of the decision context

- Clearly define the question requiring resolution
- Gather factual information from qualified experts
- Map all affected stakeholders and their interests
- Classify urgency level (Critical/Urgent/Important) to determine timeline

Phase 2: Islamic Legal Analysis

Objective: Establish the Islamic legal foundation for decision-making

- Research relevant Quranic verses, Prophetic traditions, and scholarly consensus
- Apply maqāṣid al-sharīʿah (Islamic legal objectives) framework
- Identify applicable legal maxims (qawāʿid fiqhiyyah)
- Verify that/if classical precedents address analogous situations

Phase 3: Interest Evaluation

Objective: Systematic assessment of all potential benefits and harms

- Identify and categorize all positive outcomes (benefits)
- Identify and analyze all negative consequences (harms)
- Assess probability and certainty levels for each outcome
- Evaluate immediate, medium-term, and long-term implications

Phase 4: Systematic Comparison

Objective: Rank options according to Islamic priorities and practical considerations

- Apply maqāṣid hierarchy (necessities > needs > improvements)
- Calculate net benefit for each option (benefits minus weighted harms)
- Test rankings under different scenarios (sensitivity analysis)
- Identify non-negotiable Islamic principles that cannot be compromised

Phase 5: Implementation

Objective: Execute the decision effectively with community support

- Develop stakeholder engagement and communication strategy
- Create detailed implementation plan with success metrics
- Establish risk mitigation and contingency protocols
- Document comprehensive reasoning for future reference

Phase 6: Review and Learning

Objective: Evaluate outcomes and improve future decision-making

- Assess actual results against predicted outcomes
- Document lessons learned and methodological improvements
- Share insights with other councils and scholarly community
- Conduct long-term impact evaluation

Special Procedures

Emergency Response (24-72 hours)

Abbreviated three-phase process for crisis situations:

- Rapid assessment of essential facts and Islamic principles
- Priority triage focusing on preventing irreversible harm
- Provisional decision with commitment to fuller review

Quality Assurance

- Documentation: Comprehensive reasoning records for every decision
- Appeals: Internal and external review mechanisms
- Coordination: Communication with other councils and institutions
- Continuous Improvement: Regular methodology refinement based on experience

Appendix B
Implementation Framework and Institutional Requirements for Fiqh al-Muwāzanāt

Effective deployment of the *Muwāzanāt* Decision Matrix requires standardized institutional safeguards ensuring methodological competency and procedural integrity. For Muslim American communities navigating complex political and civic engagement decisions, these implementation frameworks provide structured approaches that maintain scholarly rigor while enabling practical community guidance.

Institutional Standards and Certification

Certification criteria encompass five essential domains: verified mastery of the foundational five conditions through formal examination, institutional transparency commitments including public reasoning documentation, internal governance procedures specifying consensus thresholds and disagreement management, continuous improvement mechanisms incorporating outcome assessment, and accountability structures linking council decisions to demonstrable community welfare rather than institutional self-interest.[304]

Inter-council coordination requires systematic mechanisms balancing consistency with contextual adaptation, including regional communication networks among certified councils, comprehensive case law databases documenting *muwāzanāt* decisions and reasoning processes, structured appeal mechanisms, and periodic scholarly conferences for framework refinement.[305]

---

[304] These certification standards establish quality assurance frameworks while preventing unauthorized appropriation of the methodology's scholarly authority. Transparency commitments ensure community members can understand reasoning processes while maintaining scholarly autonomy through systematic documentation of analytical processes, textual sources, consultation participants, and reasoning justifications.

[305] The case law database system prevents duplication of analytical effort while enabling systematic development of precedents. Documentation includes final decisions, comprehensive reasoning processes, contextual factors, and outcome evaluations, creating institutional memory that enhances future decision-making efficiency while enabling appropriate adaptation to changed circumstances.

Community Engagement and Procedural Adaptations

Systematic community perspective incorporation requires structured mechanisms preserving scholarly autonomy while ensuring practical relevance. Implementation protocols include community consultation sessions, educational programming developing community understanding of *muwāzanāt* principles, systematic outcome evaluation assessing whether decisions achieve intended *maqāṣid* objectives, and periodic review processes examining practical effects on community welfare.[306]

Framework effectiveness across diverse temporal constraints requires standardized adaptation protocols maintaining analytical integrity while acknowledging practical urgency. Temporal flexibility mechanisms include abbreviated protocols for emergency community needs, explicit criteria distinguishing situations requiring full analysis from those permitting expedited approaches, and timeline templates categorizing issues by complexity and urgency.[307]

Integration with Established Scholarly Institutions

Effective implementation requires harmonious interface with existing Islamic scholarly infrastructure rather than institutional competition. Integration mechanisms encompass structured protocols incorporating guidance from established scholarly bodies into local *muwāzanāt* processes, formal communication channels with international Islamic organizations, systematic procedures reconciling framework decisions with existing *fatwā* literature, and hierarchical appeal mechanisms connecting local decisions to recognized higher scholarly authorities.[308]

---

[306] Community engagement protocols maintain appropriate boundaries between scholarly expertise and community input, ensuring popular preferences do not override sound jurisprudential analysis while ensuring scholarly reasoning addresses genuine community needs. Educational programming develops community capacity to understand and evaluate scholarly reasoning.

[307] Timeline templates include: emergency response (24-72 hours) for crisis situations; urgent community needs (2-4 weeks) for significant decisions with moderate time constraints; routine policy development (2-6 months) for comprehensive analysis; and strategic planning (6+ months) for long-term institutional development. Each category specifies appropriate analytical procedures while maintaining essential methodological integrity.

[308] Integration recognizes that local *muwāzanāt* councils operate within broader networks of Islamic scholarship and should contribute to rather than fragment scholarly discourse. Formal communication channels enable knowledge exchange with international institutions while hierarchical appeal mechanisms provide recourse when local decisions prove controversial, maintaining both local responsiveness and global scholarly coherence.

These integration efforts strengthen contemporary Islamic scholarly discourse while preserving methodological diversity and contextual adaptation appropriate to pluralistic societies, enabling Muslim American communities to maintain connection with global Islamic scholarship while developing contextually appropriate guidance for American civic and political engagement.

The implementation framework provides comprehensive infrastructure supporting systematic *muwāzanāt* methodology while maintaining scholarly integrity and community responsiveness. For Muslim American communities, these requirements provide structured approaches for developing institutional capacity to address complex contemporary challenges while maintaining connection to classical Islamic legal methodology and global scholarly discourse.

Appendix C
Addressing Fundamental Methodological Concerns in Fiqh al-Muwāzanāt

The systematization of *fiqh al-muwāzanāt* inevitably encounters objections from various quarters of Islamic scholarship, ranging from concerns about innovation (*bidʿah*) in established methodology to questions about the spiritual dimensions of Islamic legal reasoning. These concerns deserve systematic engagement rather than dismissive treatment, as they reflect legitimate anxieties about preserving the integrity and authenticity of Islamic scholarship in contemporary contexts, particularly as Muslim American communities develop sophisticated approaches to civic engagement and political participation.

Distinguishing Articulation from Legal Innovation

Traditional Islamic scholarship has maintained cautious attitudes toward methodological innovation, recognizing that changes in legal methodology can fundamentally alter substantive legal outcomes. However, Islamic intellectual history demonstrates consistent evolution in jurisprudential methodology without compromising fundamental legal principles. The development of *uṣūl al-fiqh* as a systematic discipline during the second and third Islamic centuries represents precisely this kind of methodological systematization of reasoning processes that had previously operated at intuitive levels.

Al-Shāfiʿī's "*Risālah*," widely recognized as the foundational text of Islamic legal methodology, systematized principles of analogical reasoning (*qiyās*), consensus, and textual interpretation that had previously operated without explicit methodological articulation.[309] Similarly, al-Ghazālī's "*al-Mustaṣfā*" and al-Shāṭibī's "*al-Muwāfaqāt*" represent developments that

[309] Muḥammad ibn Idrīs al-Shāfiʿī, *al-Risālah*, ed. Aḥmad Muḥammad Shākir (Cairo: Dār al-Turāth, 1979). Contemporary scholars universally recognize this systematization as methodological clarification rather than substantive innovation, establishing precedent for systematic articulation of reasoning processes previously operating without explicit methodological formulation.

articulated principles of reasoning implicit within earlier scholarly practice rather than introducing novel legal content.[310]

The distinction between methodological articulation (*bayān al-manhaj*) and substantive innovation (*iḥdāth fī al-aḥkām*) provides crucial framework for addressing innovation concerns. Explicating what was implicit does not constitute innovation, and scholars of diverse backgrounds throughout Islamic history have established a classical foundation for methodological development that clarifies rather than alters established legal reasoning. The five-condition framework proposed in this book operates according to this principle, with each condition representing systematic articulation of reasoning processes that classical scholars employed without explicit methodological formulation.

The Cultural Specificity and Complexity Objections

Some scholars argue that systematic *muwāzanāt* methodology, emerging from American Muslim experiences, reflects cultural assumptions limiting its applicability to other contexts. The framework addresses this through clear distinction between universal methodological principles and particular contextual applications. The five conditions represent universal requirements for sophisticated jurisprudential reasoning, while specific applications necessarily reflect particular circumstances.

The classical principle of "*al-ʿādah muḥakkamah*" (custom is legally authoritative) establishes that Islamic legal reasoning has always incorporated contextual considerations.[311] The *muwāzanāt* framework systematizes this integration of universal principles with contextual analysis rather than introducing novel cultural relativism. The emphasis on verification of effective cause (*taḥqīq al-manāṭ*) specifically prevents inappropriate transfer of rulings across different contexts.

---

[310] Abū Ḥāmid al-Ghazālī, *al-Mustaṣfā*. These works represent sophisticated methodological developments that articulated principles of reasoning implicit within earlier scholarly practice rather than introducing novel legal content, demonstrating the consistent evolution in jurisprudential methodology throughout Islamic intellectual history.

[311] Jalāl al-Dīn al-Suyūṭī, *al-Ashbāh wa al-Naẓāʾir fī Qawāʿid wa Furūʿ Fiqh al-Shāfiʿiyyah* (Beirut: Dār al-Kutub al-ʿIlmiyyah, 1983). This classical principle establishes that Islamic legal reasoning has always incorporated contextual considerations rather than operating through abstract universal application, providing foundation for the *muwāzanāt* framework's systematic integration of universal principles with contextual analysis while preventing inappropriate cultural relativism.

Regarding complexity concerns, the framework addresses feasibility through graduated application protocols that match analytical complexity to issue significance and available resources. The distinction between emergency response procedures, urgent community needs, and comprehensive policy development ensures appropriate scaling to practical circumstances. The systematic approach actually increases efficiency for complex issues by preventing repeated analysis and creating institutional memory for similar future issues.

Critics might argue that emphasizing post-2023 constraints in this publication reflects temporary political pessimism rather than enduring methodological insight. However, the framework's strength lies precisely in its capacity to recognize when political contexts shift from "normal" democratic competition to systematic exclusion requiring different strategic approaches. Just as classical scholars developed distinct methodologies for Muslim minorities under hostile rule versus Muslim-majority contexts, contemporary muwāzanāt must acknowledge when democratic participation occurs within fundamentally compromised systems.

The Precedent-Setting Objection: Managing Legal Precedents

Traditional Islamic scholarship has been cautious about creating legal precedents that might be inappropriately applied to future situations. The framework addresses precedent concerns through explicit documentation of reasoning processes, contextual factors, and scope limitations for each decision. Rather than creating rigid precedents, the methodology establishes transparent reasoning patterns that can be appropriately adapted to future situations.

The emphasis on *taḥqīq al-manāṭ* specifically prevents inappropriate precedent application by requiring careful analysis of whether circumstances underlying previous decisions remain applicable to new situations. The framework includes explicit review and revision procedures enabling communities to modify previous decisions when circumstances change or when experience reveals unintended consequences, enhancing rather than constraining future scholarly reasoning.

These methodological concerns reflect legitimate anxieties about preserving Islamic scholarship's integrity while developing capacity to address contemporary challenges. The systematic *muwāzanāt* framework responds to these concerns not through dismissal but through careful integration of traditional scholarship principles with structured contemporary applications. For Muslim American communities, these methodological safeguards are particularly crucial as they develop sophisticated approaches to political engagement, policy advocacy, and civic participation. The framework's emphasis on qualified scholarship, spiritual insight, contextual analysis, and precedent management provides structured approaches that honor traditional Islamic legal methodology while enabling effective engagement with contemporary American political and social contexts. The goal is not to replace traditional scholarship but to provide systematic tools that support traditional scholarly virtues, including careful analysis, spiritual insight, collective wisdom, and practical effectiveness, in addressing the complex challenges facing Muslim communities in contemporary America and beyond.

About the Author

Shaykh Dr. Suleiman Hani is a Palestinian-American international lecturer, the Dean of Academic Affairs at AlMaghrib Institute, a research fellow at Yaqeen Institute, and a leadership consultant and board adviser to numerous organizations. At the age of fourteen, he completed a Qur'an memorization program and went on to study under numerous scholars, earning dozens of traditional certifications in the Islamic sciences. He later obtained a master's degree from the University of Jordan's College of Sharīʿah, a second master's degree from Harvard University, and a doctorate in leadership from New York University. Over the past decade, he has served as a resident scholar in Michigan, lectured in over fifty countries worldwide, published several works, and appeared on major Islamic TV networks.

In addition to this book, Dr. Suleiman is the author of other popular titles:

1. 114 Tips to Help You *Finally* Memorize the Qur'an
2. Preservation of the Quran: A Brief History
3. The Iron Healing: Lessons & Reflections from Surah al-Hadid
   With 120 Discussion Questions & Mastery Tracker
4. Special Virtues of the Qur'an's Chapters & Verses
   Foreword by Dr. Omar Suleiman
5. The Golden Chain Narrations: 81 Prophetic Wisdoms Through Abdullah b. Umar (RA)
   Foreword by Mufti Muntasir Zaman
6. The Promises of Allah

For more information, visit **imamsuleiman.com**

www.ingramcontent.com/pod-product-compliance
Lightning Source LLC
Chambersburg PA
CBHW031351230926
51848CB00002B/480
* 9 7 8 1 9 6 9 3 5 8 0 3 6 *